S0-CLK-367

FINDING
◆WHAT'S◆
MISSING

FINDING WHAT'S MISSING

John Hunter

Fresh Springs Publications
Kingsport, Tennessee

Originally published as *Finding God's Best*
© 1974 Broadman Press
ISBN 0–8054–8233–4

Except where otherwise indicated, all Scripture quotations in this book are taken from the King James Version of the Bible.

Scripture quotations marked (AMP) are taken from The Amplified Bible, Old Testament. Copyright © 1965, 1987 by The Zondervan Corporation. The Amplified New Testament, copyright © 1954, 1958, 1987 by The Lockman Foundation. Used by permission.

FINDING WHAT'S MISSING

Copyright © 1995 by Fresh Springs, Inc.
Kingsport, Tennessee 37664

ISBN 1-886797-20-5

All rights reserved. No portion of this book may be reproduced in any form without the written permission of the Publisher.

Printed in the United States of America.

To my wife Ruth,

God's special gift to me.

CONTENTS

FOREWORD

Whether in his extensive Bible teaching ministry around the world, his years of affiliation with the Capernwray Missionary Fellowship, or his many writings, John Hunter has eloquently yet simply held up the Scriptures as the only true standard against which all we are and everything we do must be compared.

In a day when so many are seeking for signs and chasing after new experiences; when following what man has to say seems to be more popular than listening to what God has to say, the church is blessed to have men like Dr. John who consistently call us back to the plumbline of God's Word.

But John Hunter is not just a writer and teacher. What Patricia and I remember him most for is the warm, kind friend with whom we once traveled in ministry over England, Wales, Scotland, and Ireland. He doesn't just write about the truth; he lives it.

If *Finding What's Missing* had but one chapter, it would be more than worth your investment. If you have been living life in less than full-color, you will find between its covers truth that can lead you into the fullness of blessing God has ordained for you to enjoy in and through His Son, the Lord Jesus. That's what God wants for all of us.

Ron Owens
Office of Prayer & Spiritual Awakening
Home Mission Board, SBC

FULLNESS

"I pray that . . . you may be filled to the measure of all the fulness of God." (Eph. 17b, 19b, NIV)

One thing that the Lord requires is that we know our need of Him,
When we're hungry, when we're thirsty, when we see the awful sin
That we're bent on turning after in our search for happiness,
Fullness, fullness He has promised when we seek His righteousness.

Longing to be like the Master, He the object of our love,
Longing for the heav'nly manna that comes only from above;
To be holy, just as holy as He says we're meant to be,
Less desire for self-fulfillment, more of true humility.

But to be more like the Master we must be the kind of clay
That surrenders to the Potter as He shapes us day by day;
Learning that it is in yielding to His will, we find the key
To the secret of His fullness: It's not I, but Christ in me.

© 1989 Ron Owens
Used by permission

INTRODUCTION

In my home in England we once had an old television set, a real old-timer, almost senile in its behavior. It was a black and white set, uncertain and unsure in its performance. Sometimes it became all confused, often at the most exciting part of the program. It worked, but it presented a most unsatisfactory picture to those who were watching.

When I first saw a new, modern, color TV, I was amazed. There were the same old characters and commentators, but now they were real. I was accustomed to seeing everything in black and white—people, animals, flowers, grass, clouds, and sky—in black and white with variations of grey. But now there was color—glorious, gorgeous hues full of radiant beauty. The whole picture came to life in a new dimension.

It was the same program, but what a difference!

This is the way it is with many Christians. Some are like my old TV set—black and white, uncertain and unsure, often becoming confused at the critical moment. Others present to the world a colorful reality. Their lives are vibrant with the glow of truth. The program is the same, but what a difference!

In Isaiah 50:10 we have a graphic illustration of the same situation: "Who is among you who [reverently] fears the Lord, who obeys the voice of His Servant, yet who walks in darkness and deep trouble and has no shining splendor [in his heart]?" (AMP). There is the picture: one who walks in darkness and deep trouble with no shining splendor in his heart, the person who loves the Lord yet whose daily life is spelled out in black and white drabness, with variations of grey.

God never created a colorless world. How pitiful it would be if all sunsets were just black and white. Neither did He design a black and white Christian life. The Lord Jesus said, "I am come that they might have life, and that they might have it more abundantly" (John 10:10).

So many of us never experience this more abundant life; in fact, there are some who never enjoy life at all. They only exist in a drab world of personal failure. Something must be missing in a person's experience to produce such a deficient demonstration. How to find that "missing something" is what this book is all about.

As you read, measure yourself against the Word of God. Expose your heart to truth. Maybe you live a black and white life with "no shining splendor" in your heart.

Isaiah 50:10 goes on to give the Old Testament answer to such a condition: "Let him rely on, trust in, and be confident in the name of the Lord, and let him lean upon and be supported by his God." (AMP) There it is—rely, trust, be confident, lean on, be supported by his God. In this book we will dig deeply into these assurances and see how real they can be as shown in the Old and New Testaments, and in the day-by-day experience of the believer who has an increasing depth of involvement with the living Christ.

1

Finding the Missing Word

The massive buildup of worldwide communications is one of the characteristics of this present age. Helped by man's amazing technological inventions, the world now experiences a daily outpouring of words over the air and on the printed page, like a river in full flood. The development of the computer has brought in a new dimension to the world of words. Here they can be stored and stacked away like so many hidden, waiting enemies.

I have noticed over the past several years in my own field, the religious world, a staggering increase in the number of new books. Sometimes I wonder how the Christian bookstores are going to cope with this flood. It must be almost impossible to handle these many new titles as they keep on pouring out from the publishing houses.

In all this onrush of words from the Christian presses, I have seen a strange phenomenon: the unusual overemphasis of certain words, plus the obvious exclusion of others. For example, the word *love* has been taken and tossed around until it is worn to shreds. It has been used, abused, confused until now it has been drained of its true depth of meaning.

On the other hand, I find there is one significant

word which is missing from the vocabulary of many preachers and writers. It is a word that was of supreme importance in the Gospels and in the early church. Somehow it has slipped into the background today. Because this word and its personal involvement is missing, a whole section of truth is missing. This truth is foundational. If it is missing in the basic buildup of a Christian's faith, then whatever he erects on that limited foundation will be insecure.

Just as in the earthquake areas of California it is essential to take every possible precaution when preparing to build, so especially in these days of great moral and emotional stress it is vital that every consolidating truth should be taken into consideration when laying the foundation of our faith.

The missing word is the good old-fashioned word *repent*. This word came to past generations with all the authority of God. Men heeded it, and lives were challenged and changed. Sadly, this is not so today.

For many years I travelled worldwide, especially to the overseas mission fields, working with missionaries, national pastors, and church workers. I found the same situation that exists here in the States. In spite of all the new programs, the new techniques, the new approaches to the needs of the people, this word *repent* is conspicuous by its absence.

Once I was discussing this word with a high-school group to show the absolute and vital necessity of coming to a place of repentance in our relationship to God. When I had finished, I spoke to the youth leader and he amazed me by saying he had never considered the word *repentance*. He knew of the word, but had never recognized any need to understand it, much less to present it to his group.

In this book we are considering the missing links which cause us to live inadequate and impoverished lives. I am convinced that one of the major reasons for Christian sterility is the ignorance and non-involvement with this foundational truth summed up in the word *repentance.*

Every Christian accepts and knows the word, but it has lost its cutting edge and become neutrally ineffective. To many people the word is empty and conveys only moral overtones of possible improvement. It has assumed a negative meaning, of being sorry for what has been said or done.

And yet the true meaning of the word is clear and simple; it has never changed throughout the ages. In the Greek the verb is *metanoeo* and the noun is *metanoia.* The literal meaning is "to perceive afterwards" (from meta, which means "after," implying change, and noeo, meaning "to perceive"). It signifies a change in one's mind or purpose. In the New Testament it always involves a change for the better, an amendment, and always (except in Luke 17:3–4) a repentance from sin.

In the act of repentance a person hears certain facts. As he faces up to them, he rethinks his whole attitude to life. His thoughts lead him to a complete change of mind. He now receives a new purpose in life. His will is also brought into line with this new purpose. As a result there emerges a complete change in thought, word, and deed. This is therefore no negative word, but one packed with positive action. When a person truly repents, things are bound to happen on the inside *and* on the outside. It is true repentance that gives the authority to effective witnessing, because it reveals a turning from the old life and a turning to the will of the Lord. This act of "turning from" and "turning to" is the basic effect of repentance towards God. It is this that is missing in so many lives and, because it is missing, so much personal garbage is trailed around in day-to-day Christian living.

When the Lord Jesus restored Lazarus to Martha and Mary, as told in John's Gospel, chapter 11, he gave two commands. The first, in verse 43, was, "Lazarus, come forth." By these words he spoke to the dead man to restore his spirit, and called him forth from the tomb.

The second command was to those gathered around watching. In verse 44 we read the words, "Loose him, and let him go." Lazarus was alive, fully restored, but he could not reveal or demonstrate that life because he was hampered by his grave clothes. This is a picture of many of us today. We have life, we have been born again, but there is something vital missing from our experience. We drag around the garbage of our past lives and the graveclothes of our once dead conditions. Only a true sense of repentance can loose us and let us go!

Why is this word missing from so many vocabularies? I believe it is because of an overemphasis on another word to the neglect of the word *repent*. It is essential when presenting the gospel to press the fact that we are saved not by works of righteousness which we have done, but according to the mercy of God. We must exalt the death of Christ and present Him as the only one under heaven, given among men, whereby we must be saved. We must insist that a person's response to the mercy and love of God is to believe on the Lord Jesus Christ. At this point the word "believe" becomes of supreme importance. I must believe, for without my act of believing there is no receiving of God's goodness. This is where the danger lies, in the exclusive emphasis on the word *believe.*

In a moment we will see from the Bible that the Scriptural emphasis is "repent and believe." *First,* there has to be repentance, *then* belief. But much modern evangelism stresses the fact that "all you have to do is believe!" with no reference to repentance. This one-sided appeal may be made in honest ignorance, or it may be made to make it attractive, as a way to increase the number of those coming forward.

If all I have to do is *believe* then salvation costs me nothing. If there is no repentance then my involvement with the Lord is: Jesus *also.* I add him to the other sources of excitement in my life. I go on a "Jesus high." But if there is this act of repentance, as detailed before, then it is not Jesus *also,* but Jesus *only.*

Repentance can be a costly thing. It needs to be taken seriously. When the preacher presses the need for such a challenge, it could affect the number of decisions. Yet one of the greatest evangelists of our day, Billy Graham, always stresses the need for repentance when he makes his appeal. How often I have heard him say: "You must repent; you must turn from your old life; you must turn to Christ." It is good to see how the Lord honors the faithful preaching of the gospel.

Let us now do a simple and brief survey of the use and importance of the missing word, as shown in the New Testament.

In Mark 1:15 we read the first recorded words of the Lord Jesus: "The time is fulfilled, and the kingdom of God is at hand: repent ye, and believe the gospel." Notice the two acts called for by the Lord: *repent* and *believe.* This he presents as man's necessary response to the call of God. Notice, also, the order in which they come. First the man must repent, as we have detailed before. Then, when the act of repentance has taken place, the man goes on to believe and receive the gospel. Again, let me press this point: *if I do not become involved in the process of repentance, then I can never really fulfill the teaching of Christ, and because of this I can never enjoy the fullness of what God has for me.*

Mark 2:17 tells of a challenge to the Lord Jesus by the scribes and Pharisees. To them He gave these wonderful words: "They that are whole have no need of the physician, but they that are sick: I came not to call the righteous, but sinners to repentance." We know there are many reasons given in the Word for Christ's coming, each one adding a little more to our treasury of truth, but notice this unusual emphasis by the Lord: the purpose of His coming was *to bring sinners to repentance.* If I have not yet come to a place of repentance before the Lord—a "turning from" and a "turning to"—then I have failed Him. I, personally, have not responded to the purpose of His coming.

Mark 6:7–13 tells how the Lord sent out the twelve two by two. He instructed them in detail what to do, how to dress, what to take, how to behave, and what to say. Verse 12 tells us the main thrust of their preaching: "And they went out, and preached that men should repent." Notice how limited was their ministry. The people to whom they preached were religious; they believed in the one true God. But before even the Lord could present His truth, there needed to be the preparation of repentance.

Luke 15 contains a two-fold comment by the Lord. I never really appreciated the truth of what He said until some time ago. This chapter contains the stories of the lost sheep, the lost coin, and the lost son. In verse 7 the

Lord said: "I say unto you, that likewise joy shall be in heaven over one sinner that repenteth, more than over ninety and nine just persons, which need no repentance." Then in verse 10 we read: "Likewise, I say unto you, there is joy in the presence of the angels of God over one sinner that repenteth." Notice the unusual comment on angelic behavior. Be sure you see what it is that makes the angels rejoice. I used to assume that they had joy when someone believed, but this is not what Jesus said. He specifically stated twice that what brought joy in heaven was the *repentance* of a sinner, not necessarily his believing.

A popular concept of salvation is that when I believe in Christ and accept Him as my own personal Savior then my *standing* is changed. I no longer am a sinner dead in my sins. I am born again. I am a new creature in Christ, and I have a new destination. Heaven is my home.

But salvation includes repentance. When I truly repent and believe, then not only is my *standing* changed; my *state* is changed. I "turn from" and I "turn to," and my whole behavior is changed. Not only do I have the belief, I have the behavior to back it up. Not only is my destination changed; I have a new destiny here on earth. I can be what I have become—a new creature in Christ.

This is what gives joy to the angels. They want to see the behavior; they want to know it is real.

This may be where you need to double check once more. Have you repented *and* believed, or have you only believed? Have you given joy to the angels yet? What a challenge! This could be one of the reasons why you have no shining splendor in your heart.

Luke 24 is the chapter of resurrection. The Lord we meet there is the risen, victorious Christ speaking to His own. In verses 44–49 He speaks words of unusual and vital importance in which He reordains and recommissions His disciples for their future life's work. In verse 47 the Lord specifically stated what was to be their ministry: "And that repentance and remission of sins should be preached in His name among all nations, beginning at Jerusalem." Notice that He told them where they had to begin, in Jerusalem, and where they had to go, among all nations. Notice in particular what the message was to be: repentance and remission of sins. I find this to be a most challenging statement. Here is the risen Lord telling what had to be said and where; but somehow we have missed out on that first word, repentance. We are most careful to preach the cross and forgiveness of sins by believing in Christ, but where is the repentance?

Look now in the book of Acts and see how faithfully the early church obeyed the Lord. Acts 2 records the first sermon ever preached by Peter, on the day of Pentecost. There was a great spirit of conviction in the hearts of his hearers. Later on that same day about three thousand souls were going to be added to their number. Verse 37 records their reaction to the message. "Now when they heard this, they were pricked in their heart, and said unto Peter and to the rest of the apostles, Men and brethren, what shall we do?" Notice now the reaction of Peter. He did not do as many would do today: he did not call them to the front, get them to fill in a form, then count up the extent of the blessing. Verse 38 gives his answer: "Then Peter said unto them, Repent, and be baptized every one of you in the name of Jesus Christ for the remission of sins, and ye shall receive the gift of the Holy Ghost." What precious things were promised then and there—baptism, remission of sins, the Holy Spirit—

but see how it all began with that same key word, repent.

Acts 3 records the incident of Peter and John on their way to the Temple meeting and healing the man who was lame from birth. It tells how the crowd gathered and how Peter took the opportunity to witness for the Lord. Verse 19 shows how he applied the truth to their hearts, challenging them to make a response: "Repent ye therefore, and be converted, that your sins may be blotted out." Once more Peter was faithful to the instructions of his risen Lord Who had said that repentance and remission of sins should be preached, beginning in Jerusalem.

In Acts 17 we have the words of another preacher, speaking to another race of people. Verse 19 tells how certain philosophers in Athens took Paul to the Areopagus, saying, "May we know what this new doctrine, whereof thou speakest, is?" The succeeding verses give an account of Paul's speech. Verse 30 tells how Paul clinched his message by challenging his hearers: "And the times of this ignorance God winked at; but now commandeth all men everywhere to repent."

I find this to be a most remarkable statement for several reasons. First, it was to pagans; previously the challenge had come to the Jews. Then the Holy Spirit detailed three things: God commands repentance, to all men, everywhere. *The call to repentance is not a selective option; it is an act commanded by God.* So if I have not repented, either by ignorance or by choice, then I have gone deliberately against the will of God as revealed consistently in His Word.

In Acts 20 we read some heart-searching words from the lips of Paul. He was on his way back to Jerusalem. There was a deep sense of urgency in his haste. Verse

17 tells how he made his last contact with the church at Ephesus: "And from Miletus he went to Ephesus, and called the elders of the church." What followed was full of sorrow and pathos as he reviewed his ministry among them. Verses 20 and 21 give a summary of all that Paul had accomplished—his method and his ministry: "I kept back nothing that was profitable unto you, but have shewed you, and have taught you publicly, and from house to house, testifying both to the Jews, and also to the Greeks, repentance toward God, and faith toward our Lord Jesus Christ."

Notice why he taught this (because it was profitable); where he taught it (publicly and from house to house); and to whom he taught it (both to Jews and Greeks). Then be sure you realize what Paul's basic message was: repentance toward God and faith toward our Lord Jesus Christ. Once again Paul was completely faithful to the commands of the risen Christ. Through all the years he preached at Ephesus, his ministry to saint and sinner began with the essential word, repent.

Finally, look in Acts 25. This is one of the most colorful scenes in the life of Paul. Verse 23 paints the picture: "And on the morrow, when Agrippa was come, and Bernice, with great pomp, and was entered into the place of hearing, with the chief captains, and principal men of the city, at Festus' commandment Paul was brought forth." There was Paul, all alone, facing the pomp and power of Rome, witnessing to the truth of his conversion and also to his response to the commandment of the risen Christ:

> "Whereupon, O king Agrippa, I was not disobedient unto the heavenly vision: but

shewed first unto them of Damascus, and at Jerusalem, and throughout all the coasts of Judaea, and then to the Gentiles, that they should repent and turn to God, and do works meet for repentance" (Acts 26:19–20).

See how Paul is giving the historical and geographical sequence of his whole life's ministry—Damascus, Jerusalem, Judaea, the Gentiles. In other words, this is the way Paul preached wherever he went; it is also *what* he preached. Again the same emphasis is there: repentance, plus works meet for repentance. He expected to see changed lives based on a "turning from" and a "turning to."

I am challenged when I hear Paul say, "I was not disobedient unto the heavenly vision." Obedience involved preaching repentance. If he had omitted this costly challenge to the lives of his hearers, he would have been disobedient to the living Lord.

We know that the preaching of the early church turned the world upside down. Lives were changed and there was a demonstration of power such as the world had never seen before or has seen since. Much of this success must have come from the faithful, obedient preaching of repentance. And yet, this is the word which is missing from our present evangelical vocabulary.

Surely this must be one of the reasons why so many lives are drab and powerless, why there is "no shining splendor" such as shone in the hearts and lives of the little nobodies of the early church.

God still commands it. It is still disobedience not to preach it. Why not check your own heart and see what God would have you do?

2

Finding the Missing Experience

Over the years I have had many opportunities to counsel with people—in churches, colleges, and conferences, at home and overseas. Invariably, one of the comments made is that there is something missing in their Christian lives. Sometimes it is an experience they once enjoyed but which has now gone. With others it is a sense of the need of something more than what they experience at the present.

In one sense this can be a healthy sign, like that of a baby seeking food and nourishment, a very natural thing to do. Whatever the cause, it all adds up to the same thing: the search for the missing experience. It is good to know that there is an answer to this search, one that can completely satisfy all the longings of the human heart.

The final answer is stated for us in Colossians 2:8–10 where the Holy Spirit is exalting the person of Christ:

> "Beware lest any man spoil you through philosophy and vain deceit, after the tradition of men, after the rudiments of the world, and not after Christ. For in him dwelleth all the fulness of the Godhead bodily. And ye are complete in him, which is the head of all principality and power."

What magnificent words these are: In Christ dwells all the fullness of the Godhead bodily. All that there is in God is in Christ! Then the equally amazing statement: You are complete in Him. *You are complete in Him!*

It is the last phrase which has so gripped my mind. I am complete in Christ! Just consider this statement for a moment. We have been talking about people who feel there is something missing in their lives, and here is the Word of God telling us we are complete in Christ. If a thing is complete, then nothing is missing.

Notice also the tense used in this phrase—you *are* complete in Christ, not, you will be! Truly there are many more glorious experiences awaiting us in the future when we are with Him forevermore, but this phrase talks of a quality of completeness here and now. As I go on into all the issues of life—its joys, sorrows, victories, and failures—I am complete in Christ.

This does not say that I experience that completeness. Many of us, as we have seen, are very conscious of something missing in our lives. But in one sense it should put an end to our search for completeness. We now know where it is: in Christ.

No new program, new look, or new gimmick can produce that completeness. No new baptism, no new spiritual, charismatic involvement can produce that completeness, because I already am complete—in Christ. My need is to work out the completeness that He already has worked into my life.

Again, referring to past counseling experiences, I have met with people who on some previous occasions were sure they had found what was missing in their lives. Because of their newfound certainty they had plunged into this new area which promised satisfaction. Each one eventually had come up with the same conclusion:

However much it may have promised that complete satisfaction, when they finally put it to the test, it failed.

No one should be surprised at this. If completeness could be found in a thing, an experience, an organization, then Christ would be a failure, because He could not, of Himself, provide for a full and complete satisfaction for the human heart.

Let the simplicity of this glorious statement fill and thrill your soul. You are, here and now, complete in Christ. You need nothing more and no one more. The great question is, of course, how can I experience this sense of completeness? This is what we are going to consider now.

Romans 5 is a great and glorious exposition of Christian truth. I want us to consider it first of all in its historical setting. It was written, originally, to a group of "little nobodies" who made up the church in Rome. Spiritually they were part of the body of Christ, but physically they were part of the great and mighty Roman Empire. As such, they were caught in the web of the soul-less, soul-destroying structure we know as the Roman way of life.

Gibbon, in his authoritative study of the Roman Empire, tells us that there were more than fifty million slaves in bondage in this social system. Actually, half of the people in the vast structure were slaves. A man could be a medical doctor, a schoolmaster, a business executive, and still be a slave. As a slave he owned nothing and had no rights. He received no wages and was on call twenty-four hours a day, seven days a week, and fifty-two weeks a year. If he was married, his wife and children belonged to another man, and they could be disposed of separately without his consent.

A Roman farmer, when taking stock on his farm

would list the number of four-legged animals, then the number of two-legged animals. These latter would be men and women held in the bondage of slavery. Slaves were classed as "things." Just imagine the soul-destroying thought of being simply a "thing," a nonhuman!

Many of those in the early Christian church were slaves. It is easy to see how the all-embracing, all-comforting teaching of the gospel would appeal to them in their abject lowliness.

With these thoughts in mind, turn now to Romans 5:1–5 and see a picture of people who belonged to that culture. As we read, notice the quality of the lives they lived. In one sense, this is a setting forth of the phrase we have considered. They were complete in Christ, and they demonstrated that completeness day by day in every walk of life. Measure your own life against the lives of these nobodies, and test your capacity for completeness against their experience.

Verse 1 begins with condition of faith, and the consequence of faith: "Therefore being justified by faith, we have peace with God through our Lord Jesus Christ." This is how we, too, came to Christ. We also were justified by faith—the only condition of blessing. But now notice the following wonderful words: *we have peace*. These dear people had a quality of peace that mystified and challenged the Roman world. In the midst of all their pressures and sufferings they enjoyed the peace of God which passed all understanding. This is not so with many of the Lord's people these days. Those with whom I counsel come to me because they have no peace. In fact, real peace is a missing commodity in the world today—internationally, nationally, domestically, and in the business world, as well as in the hearts of many believers.

Once a Christian psychiatrist shared with me his concern over the fact that so many Christians now run to psychiatrists for help. Certainly, there are those who need professional and medical assistance. But he said the majority of those inquiring knew little or nothing of their resources in Christ. If I am complete in Christ, then I am complete in sorrow, in tragedy, in bereavement, in any situation.

Verse 2 tells us more of their demonstration of completeness: "By whom also we have access by faith into this grace wherein we stand, and rejoice in hope of the glory of God." Notice, once more, that all they possessed was by faith. Realize that God has no favorites. He never gave them more than He gives us. The great difference in our lives is what we do with that which God gives us.

Two things are stated here which characterized their lives: *we stand, we rejoice.* The word *stand* is a special word. It presents a picture of a Roman soldier in all his armor standing strong and firm to face the foe. This is one of the things missing from many Christian lives these days. So many people don't stand firm and face up to the situation. They run and hide. They take evasive action, anything to avoid confrontation with the unwanted situation. They do this because they haven't the strength to stand, and yet our phrase tells us they are complete in Christ.

Some years ago I was in Vietnam, in Dalat, working with the tribal people in the village of Sutong. The day before my arrival, Viet Cong guerrillas had shot and killed a young man of that village. The tribal pastor came to Dalat to give the news to John Newman in whose home I was staying. John translated for me what the pastor said. He spoke of the young man's parents, how they had trusted Christ over twenty years ago in the mountains. He told of sufferings and tragedies that had filled their lives. He recounted how they had lost eleven children, and now this was the twelfth bereavement in their family. They had only one child left, and he was a helpless cripple. Then the pastor, overcome with grief and compassion, tried to describe how the parents were facing this bitter blow. He said, "They are standing, standing, like . . . a tree!" He was searching for an appropriate simile, and he found it. Standing like a tree! Tossed in the storms, branches broken, battered and bewildered, yet it stood firm because the roots were deep in the solid rock.

This is the meaning of the word in verse 2. We stand. We can take it, not because of who we are, but because of who Christ is, and because we are complete in Him.

The second thing said about the early believers in verse 2 is, *we rejoice.* This is something of great importance these days. These people had a capacity for joy. Two of the emotions we can experience are happiness and joy. A Christian should enjoy both. Happiness happens. It comes and goes. It depends upon our circumstances. Happiness is a surface reaction, just as a lake reflects the lights and shadows of the passing clouds. But joy is something deep down in the human heart, completely independent of circumstances. When a storm rages at sea, the waves are tossed to and fro and the surface of the sea presents a picture of utter confusion. But not too far below the surface there is peace. There the water is at rest, untroubled by the violence of the storm above. This is the way joy operates. Conditions around us may be unlovely and unwanted, but deep down in the heart which is complete in Christ, which is resting in Him, there is a joy that nothing can take away or destroy. These dear people in the early church had peace. They could stand like a tree. They had joy in all the storms of life.

Verse 3 adds more information to the quality of their lives: "And not only so, but we glory in tribulations also: knowing that tribulation worketh patience." They could find glory in the midst of tribulation. What a challenge! We can learn much from the word *tribulation*. It is a picture word; its origin describes its meaning. It comes from *tribulum,* a Roman agricultural implement used in threshing wheat. It consisted of two poles linked together by a leather hinge. The men using these tools stood around a heap of ears of wheat. Each man in turn swung his tribulum back, then over his head. As the loose pole reached its apex, it beat down on the wheat, separating the grain from the chaff. So the act of threshing was a series of blows rained down on the one place. This is what tribulation is—blow after blow, all falling on the one life. No bones are broken, no blood is shed, just the sense of a build-up of pressure and crushing sorrow.

How true this must have been in the lives of many of those in the early church. And yet they found glory in the midst of their tribulation. We can link this phrase with Colossians 1:27. Here the Holy Spirit speaks of God's plan for our day-by-day Christian lives: ". . . the riches of the glory of this mystery . . ." What amazing words! All the possibility of blessing is based on one glorious truth: Christ in you, the hope of glory. Realize that the glory referred to here is not the future glory of heaven, but a hope of glory here and now based on the indwelling Christ. This is part of what it means to be complete in Him. This is the experience so sadly missing from so many lives today. The glory these early

Christians found in all their tribulation was the sheer joy of knowing, and proving, the truth of the One who said: "I will never leave thee, nor forsake thee" (Heb. 13:5).

The purpose of the tribulum was to separate the wheat from the chaff. This it did for the Roman farmer. In a much more wonderful way this is also what tribulation can do in the heart and life of a Christian. As I recognize the presence and power of Christ in my sorrows and count upon my completeness in Him, there comes a separation in my own life of the wheat and the chaff. That which is good and of true value is seen standing firm; that which is useless dross in my life is shown up in its true colors. This is why the lives of the early Christians sparkle with a sense of wondrous power and rich goodness.

The continuing verses in Romans 5 detail the quality of life that proceeds from this capacity to find glory in the midst of tribulation: ". . . knowing that tribulation worketh patience; And patience, experience; and experience, hope: And hope maketh not ashamed; because the love of God is shed abroad in our hearts by the Holy Ghost which is given unto us." (vv. 3b–5).

What a fine procession of sterling qualities—patience, experience, hope—all leading to a life which is unashamed. Notice in particular the words that tie up the whole sequence: "because the love of God is shed abroad in our hearts by the Holy Ghost which is given unto us." All this is possible through the indwelling Holy Spirit. When we realize that the Lord Jesus Christ indwells us in the person of His Holy Spirit, we can see once more the great truth: we are complete in Him.

This then is the quality of life set forth by the early Christians. How does your life measure up with theirs?

Do you have that rare peace? Do you stand like a tree? Is there real joy? Can you find glory in tribulation and does all this lead on to patience, experience, and hope? I find that with many of us today we come nowhere near that standard of Christian living. Would you like to know the secret of their success? Would you be interested in following their example?

If we go on to look into verses 8–10 we will find not only the secret of their success but the way in which we, too, can go on to live out day by day the glorious completeness which is ours in Christ. These three verses tell us the three tenses of our salvation through the Lord Jesus.

Verse 8 gives us the past tense: "But God commendeth his love toward us, in that, while we were yet sinners, Christ died for us." This verse tells me of the forgiveness of my sins because Christ died for me, as we read in 1 Peter 3:18: "For Christ also hath once suffered for sins, the just for the unjust, that he might bring us to God." This is the finished work of Christ, one sacrifice for sins, forever. Notice that this forgiveness is mine because of the death of Christ. I am saved by His death.

You will have recognized that most of my quotations are from the King James translation. I am using it because I enjoy it. I was brought up with it. I memorized from its pages and it speaks to me with clarity, forthrightness, and dignity. There are occasions also when the arrangement of words and phrases adds extra emphasis to the meaning. This is very apparent in the next two verses.

Verse 8 told us the wonder of sins forgiven through the death of Christ. There are some poor folk who believe that is *all* they can be sure of. They speak wistfully about eternal security, they hope they will be in heaven, but they have no real assurance. Verse 9 in the King James speaks out with strong conviction: "Much more then, being now justified by his blood, we shall be saved from wrath through him." Notice those two opening words: *much more*. There is much more than sins forgiven; there is the certainty of being saved from wrath. This is the future tense of my salvation. Once more, it is mine because of the death of Christ. I am saved by His death.

Having discussed the certainty of sins forgiven and a home in heaven, all available through the death of Christ, I am well aware that this is what many Christians would call the extent of their salvation. This is how I was saved when in my early twenties. They said to me such words as: "Now, young man you are saved, your sins are forgiven, you have a home in heaven. Now out you go and live for Jesus." I knew so little, it all sounded so right, and that is exactly what I did—I set out to live for Jesus. My salvation had a past tense and a future tense. I set out to work out the present tense. This is the way it is with so many of us. We are sincere, we try our best to live for Jesus. When we fail, we feel guilty and work harder to fulfill our hopes. But, of course, we never can really live for Jesus. The Bible never commands or expects it. We eventually end up by accepting a defeated Christian life as the normal thing. This is all we see in most of the Christians around us.

But the Word says we are complete in Christ; all that I need is in Christ. I don't have to be a failure. The Christians in the early Church were not failures. As we have seen, they lived gloriously complete lives. How did they do it? Mainly because they experienced the truth in verse 10: "For if, when we were enemies, we were reconciled to God by the death of his Son, much more, being reconciled, we shall be saved by his life."

This is one of the key verses in the Bible. This verse changed my Christian life when I suddenly realized it was talking about another kind of salvation. We have seen so far, in verse 8, the past tense of our salvation, and in verse 9, the future tense. Both of these were won for us through the death of Christ. Knowing these two facts is called, in the Bible, being reconciled to God. We are the guilty ones, we were the enemies, but as verse 10 says, we were reconciled to God by the death of His Son.

Now notice the next two words in verse 10—*much more*. This is how the truth struck me one day as I considered this verse. There is much more in God's salvation than having sins forgiven and a home in heaven. This was the thing I had never realized before. This is what so many Christians have never yet realized. God has more for us than reconciliation . He does not just forgive us, promise us a home in heaven, and then send us on our way to struggle as best we can. God does not ask us to live for Jesus; neither does He expect it.

The inner secret of God's plan for us is in the continuing words in verse 10: *"Much more, being reconciled, we shall be saved by His life."* There it is. Because we are reconciled, and that by the death of Christ, we can now go on to be saved by His life. Don't miss this tremendous statement, *saved by His life*. This, in a sense, is the other half of God's salvation, the other side of the coin of salvation. We are saved through the *death* of Christ. This is the finished work of Christ—sins forgiven and a home in heaven. We are also saved by the *life* of Christ; this is the unfinished, unfolding work of Christ.

The Amplified Bible translates it this way: ". . . we shall be saved [daily delivered from sin's dominion] through His [resurrection] life." God's salvation is a present tense, daily delivered from sin's dominion, from the pressure of daily life, from fear, worry, and anxiety, from guilt and failure. I can be saved from all these through the risen life of Christ. Where is the risen Christ today? He is seated at the right hand of the Father. It is wonderful to realize there is a man in heaven. But that isn't all. Second Corinthians 13:5 has some challenging words on this subject: "Examine yourselves, whether ye be in the faith; prove your own selves. Know ye not your own selves, how that Jesus Christ is in you, except ye be reprobates?" The last word, *reprobates,* means fakes, outcasts, rejects.

Notice how personal this verse is—yourselves, your own selves, *your own selves.* This teaches us that the proof of being in the faith is that the Lord Jesus is in us. He personally indwells every believer in the person of His Holy Spirit. This is where the risen life of Christ is—in the heart and life of the Christian.

In other words, I do not have to live for Jesus. He who indwells me wants to live in me, and for me, and through me! This was something I never realized for years. This may be your great area of failure. You may be seeking so earnestly to live for Him when, all the time, He is seeking to take over in your life and live for you.

This was the experience of those Christians in the early church. This is why they had peace, could stand like trees, had joy, found glory in tribulation, developed patience, experience, and hope. Paul could say: "For to me to live is Christ" (Phil. 1:21); "I can do all things through Christ which strengtheneth me" (Phil. 4:13).

This is how we are complete in Christ. Whether or not we realize it we as believers are indwelt by the risen Christ. He indwells us so that He can continue in our daily lives what He began through His death on the cross. By the *saving death* of Christ, He is *the sin-bearer.* Through the *saving life* of Christ, He is *the burden-bearer.* There are so many Christians today struggling hard to live the Christian life, facing problems, and bearing burdens God never intended them to bear.

Realize in a new way that the missing experience in your life is failure to become involved with the glorious truth: You are complete in Him. You are complete, but you only experience completeness when you take a complete Christ—both His saving death and His saving life.

Coming to the cross is most wonderful and precious. I receive forgiveness of sins and a home in heaven. But coming to the cross isn't all God has for us. We need to come to the Christ, day by day and hour by hour. If I only take half of what God offers, then I can only enjoy half a salvation! Sure, my sins are forgiven and I have a home in heaven, but that is only half of my salvation.

God has more, so much more for us through our personal relationship with the risen indwelling Christ. Does this make sense to you? Would you like to know the risen Christ real in your daily life?

A Prayer of Realization

Heavenly Father, I thank you for your greatness, your majesty, and your glory. I thank you for your glorious plan of salvation and for your inspired Word which teaches that plan.

I thank you for the two-fold offer of the Lord Jesus as my Savior. I thank you for His precious death on the cross whereby I receive forgiveness of sins and a home in heaven. I also thank you for His risen life. Although I cannot begin to understand how, I thank you that the Lord Jesus indwells me through His Holy Spirit.

Lord Jesus, I thank you for all your promises: that you will never leave me nor forsake me, that you are with me always. Help me now to accept this in a new and vital way.

May I realize that you still are my Savior, that I do not have to live for you or struggle on my own to cope with all the pressures of life.

Lord Jesus, here and now I yield to you the daily running of my life. Be pleased to take over and live Your life through me. May I go on to know true peace, to stand like a tree, to have true joy, to find the glory of Your presence in all my sorrow and tribulation—to *experience* completeness in Christ.

All this I ask, expecting nothing but your blessing, because I ask it in Your name and for Your glory.

Amen.

3

Finding the Missing Success

What does the word *success* mean to you? An excellent, secure job, a good home, plenty of money, a happy family, good health, no problems with the children, all the things you ever wanted? All these things are good, and very desirable, and there is nothing whatever wrong in seeking them. But, if you could achieve satisfaction in each area, would that be real success?

I say this because I meet people who apparently have everything they ever dreamed of and yet are not satisfied. Real success has eluded them. Just a few weeks ago I counseled with a man during a series of meetings. I did not know it at the time, but this man was a millionaire several times over. How spiritually hungry he was, how eager to receive Christ as his Savior! What a joy to see the look and to sense the deep satisfaction filling his heart as this man came to a real sense of Christ living in his life.

But, wonderful though that was, only time will show whether he really has achieved success in life, because experience shows that many true Christians fail to find it. They are never able to turn their belief into behavior. Accustomed to the world's way of thinking, they expect success to be a positive experience; they look for things to be bigger and better. If their hopes do not materialize, then they feel they have failed and their lives become shadowed with despondency.

This is especially true in our churches. Pastors, Christian workers, deacons, elders, and church members expect the church to increase in numbers and to multiply in its organizational outreach. One sure sign of success is the building of new educational facilities or the erection of a new sanctuary to hold the greatly increased congregation. All this, plus duplicate services, is spoken of as success.

Thank God for every outward sign of an increased involvement! But is this real success, the way the Bible spells it out?

The previous chapter took us to Romans 5, as we discussed the wonder of being complete in Christ. One of the things we noted was the use of the two words, *much more*. There was much more than sins forgiven; there was a home in heaven. There was much more than being reconciled to God; there was the reality of being daily delivered by the risen, victorious life of Christ as He indwells us.

In this same chapter in Romans there is another much more. You may say, "How can there be much more than experiencing completeness in Christ?" We will see that this other much more leads on to finding the missing success apparent in many lives today. It deals with the mechanics of Christian living.

Verse 17 reads: "For if by one man's offense death reigned by one; much more they which receive abundance of grace and of the gift of righteousness shall reign in life by one, Jesus Christ." The much more discussed here is the ability to *reign in life*. This is a most penetrating phrase. The Bible teaches that there are many wonderful experiences awaiting us in the life to come. Second Timothy 2:12 says: "If we suffer, we shall also reign with him." Revelation 5:10, speaking of the future says: "And hast made us unto our God kings and priests: and we shall reign on the earth." Revelation 20:4,6 speak of those who shall reign with Christ a thousand years.

All of these last references speak of the future and refer to reigning after death; but this verse in Romans speaks of reigning, here and now, in *life*. The actual meaning of the word is: "to be a king," in control of the situation. Just consider for a moment what the Bible really says and what is God's plan for those who become involved with this much more.

This reigning is no temporary experience, no thrill for a moment. This is not talking about everything going well, about freedom from problems and frustrations. This is presenting the tremendous fact of being in control of any and every situation. Whatever problems, difficulties, tragedies, or sorrows may come, the "much more" person has the power and the ability to reign at that time in that situation. But notice the one condition: "shall reign in life by one, Jesus Christ." The power to do all this is vested in one Person, the Lord Jesus!

The person who enjoys this experience is so united and involved with the Lord that, through that same Lord, he can be in control and stay in control. This is what the Bible calls success.

Consider the ministry of our Lord here on earth. In the eyes of the world the cross was the ultimate in failure, and Jesus' whole life was a wasted effort. But in the eyes of heaven what appeared to be failure was the greatest success this world has ever known. Why was this so? Because Christ was in control of the whole situation. In the garden of Gethsemane, when the great multitude came to arrest Jesus, Peter attacked the enemy to defend his Lord. But Jesus told Peter there were twelve legions of angels ready and waiting to come to His aid. A Roman legion consisted of six thousand men, so seventy-two thousand angels were on hand, but He did not need them.

All through His life the Lord was always in control—among the sick, facing evil spirits, in the midst of the storm, cleansing the Temple. Even at the very moment of His death He was in control. John 19:30, speaking of the death of Christ, reads: "When Jesus therefore had received the vinegar, he said, It is finished: and he bowed his head, and gave up the ghost." The phrase *He bowed His head* actually means a deliberate putting of the head into a position of rest. True, He suffered and bled and died, and in His humanity every agony was intensified. But He was not only the Son of God, He was God the Son, and as such He was in control.

Romans 5:17 speaks of the believer, so united with Christ, that he, too, can experience the wonder of reigning in life. Paul describes this capacity to be in control in 2 Corinthians 4:8–11. Notice the difficult circumstances in which he was placed, but see his success in those conditions, and notice how and why all this was possible:

> "We are troubled on every side, yet not distressed; we are perplexed, but not in despair: Persecuted, but not forsaken; cast down, but not destroyed; Always bearing about in the body the dying of the Lord Jesus, that the life of Jesus might be made manifest in our body.

> For we which live are always delivered unto death for Jesus' sake, that the life also of Jesus might be made manifest in our mortal flesh."

This is real success, a man reigning in life; but notice the secret for success: *that the life also of Jesus might be made manifest in our mortal flesh.* Paul indeed reigned in life, but it was by one Jesus Christ. The Lord Jesus lived in Paul in the person of His Holy Spirit, just as He indwells every born-again believer. Paul's success came because the life of Jesus was made manifest in his mortal flesh. Our problem is that so often it is the life of "me" which comes through. And yet God has no favorites. He did not give Paul any more than He gives us. What mattered was what Paul did with what God gave him!

Look back at the verse in Romans 5 and see now who these people are who reign in life by one Jesus Christ. Notice there is no reference to age, sex, color, social status, education, or theological training. The verse tells us the simple fact that: "they which receive abundance of grace and of the gift of righteousness shall reign." In order to achieve this success, I must have received two gifts from God: abundance of grace and the gift of righteousness.

Let us look at these gifts in turn. Maybe you will discover why you cannot reign in life, and maybe you will put it right. Look first at the last of the two, the gift of righteousness. This is something that every true Christian already has received. When we come to the cross as sinners, we come seeking forgiveness and cleansing. As we confess our sins, repent of our sins, and turn from our sins, we accept the Lord Jesus as our own personal Savior, and we are accepted in Him. According to the promise of God, our sins are forgiven and we are cleansed. There is a glorious sense of freedom from the burden and guilt of sin. But that is not all that God does for us.

It is wonderful to be forgiven and cleansed, but then God does one thing more. He does not leave us cleansed and in our human nakedness before Him. He clothes us in the righteousness of Christ, so that instead of the garment of our sins we wear the robe of His righteousness. This is the gift of righteousness mentioned in Romans 5:17. When God looks at us He sees the righteousness of His beloved Son. We are accepted in the beloved. Revelation 7:9 speaks of this glorious dress: "After this I beheld, and, lo, a great multitude, which no man could number, of all nations, and kindreds, and people, and tongues, stood before the throne, and before the Lamb, clothed with white robes, and palms in their hands." The remaining verses in the chapter tell of the white robes: ". . . they have washed their robes, and made them white in the blood of the Lamb." (v. 14b). They tell also of the final blessing to come.

This, then, is the gift of righteousness which is ours through the death of Christ, His saving death. Every believer is so blessed. But receiving this one gift does not qualify us to reign in life. There are many true Christians who have been blessed this way, but their lives demonstrate nothing but their own failure. There is one more gift to be received to enable me to enjoy the missing success—the abundance of grace.

As believers we know that we are saved by grace. Ephesians 2:8–9 tells us so: "For by grace are ye saved through faith; and that not of yourselves: it is the gift of God: Not of works, lest any man should boast."

We receive grace at the cross, thus ensuring our salvation. Now here is the problem: I meet many people who truly are saved, and who know they are saved by the grace of God, but in one sense the moment of their salvation was the only time they consciously became involved with the grace of God. Having been saved by grace through the saving death of Christ, they then went on to live out their newfound life by works.

In other words, these people never have received *abundance* of grace; they have only received grace at the cross. Receiving abundance of grace is a day-by-day, moment-by-moment activity, like breathing. I continue to receive the abundance of God's grace when I become involved with the saving life of Christ as we saw in the previous chapter in this book.

Romans 5:10 tells us the glorious fact that we could be daily delivered from sin's dominion by His resurrection life. I can only experience this day-by-day deliverance as I recognize the other half of my salvation, the saving life of Christ. As I yield to Him and open my heart and life to His risen power, then once more the grace of God flows in living power through my life. As I continue to make Him real in my life and Lord of my life, then I continue to receive the abundance of grace as mentioned in verse 17.

This is how a Christian is able to reign in life by one, Jesus Christ. Through His death and precious shed blood we receive the gift of righteousness, and through His indwelling Holy Spirit we *continue to receive* the abundance of grace.

This is what Paul was saying when he spoke about the life of Jesus being made manifest through his mortal flesh. It was the Christ Who indwelt Paul that enabled him to find continuing success in the tragedies and testings of his life. In connection with those verses in 2 Corinthians 4, make sure you realize that Paul did not make the life of Jesus manifest. Paul did not have to be a little Jesus, or a copy of Jesus. In Philippians 1:21, he said: "For to me to live is Christ." He was not imitating Christ or following His example, but just allowing the Lord to be Himself in Paul's yielded life.

This truth is brought home to us again in Hebrews 3. Here the Holy Spirit speaks to other hearers, but His message sounds very much the same. Notice to whom the words are written. Verse 1 says: "Wherefore, holy brethren, partakers of the heavenly calling." These were true believers; they had responded to the call of God; they had received the gift of righteousness; and they thus were holy brethren.

But now notice what the Spirit says in verse 12: "Take heed, brethren, lest there be in any of you an evil heart of unbelief, in departing from the living God." These are the same people as in verse 1, *holy brethren, partakers of the heavenly calling*, but they are in danger. Even though they are true believers, they still can be guilty of having an evil heart of unbelief. This phrase refers to the unbelief of the believer, and it tells quite simply how such a condition can arise: by departing from the living God. The Amplified Bible puts it this way: "[Therefore beware], brethren, take care lest there be in any one of you a wicked, unbelieving heart [which refuses to cleave to, trust in and rely on Him] leading you to turn away and desert or stand aloof from the living God."

Make sure the full impact of this truth is clear to you. These were believers, people who already have been saved by the death of Christ, but now they were in danger for one reason only—that of refusing to trust in and rely on the living God! They had trusted in the saving death, but they were not trusting in the saving life. To describe the condition the Bible uses very strong language: *"lest there be in any of you a wicked unbelieving heart."*

These people knew about the saving life of Christ, as He indwelt them, but they were in danger of turning their backs on God's glorious provision and going their own way.

Many Christians today are not deliberately following that pattern of behavior. With many, their way of life is the result of honest ignorance. They know about the cross, and salvation from sins, and a home in heaven, but no one has ever told them about the reality of the indwelling Christ and why He is there. It was this way in my life for many years.

Nevertheless, deliberate or in ignorance, the result is the same, a departure from all that is available through the indwelling Christ and choosing to do "what is right in their own eyes."

Verse 13 tells what happens to the Christian who goes that way: "But exhort one another daily, while it is called Today; lest any of you be hardened through the deceitfulness of sin." If I continue to run my life my own way, then I will be deceived. In the original text the word *deceive* means to cheat or to beguile. It implies that which gives a false impression, whether by appearance, statement, or influence. As I go my own way, making my own choices, I deceive myself and cheat myself out of the blessing awaiting me. In doing so I become hardened. I cease to be responsive to the will of God. I do not have a tender conscience eager to sense the guidance of the Spirit.

Then verse 14 tells us how to put the whole thing

right. Here is divine wisdom for the divine way: "For we are made partakers of Christ, if we hold the beginning of our confidence stedfast unto the end." We continue to partake of Christ if we maintain our confidence in Him, the same kind of confidence we had at the beginning.

Can you see how this truth ties in perfectly with the words in Romans 5:17? Those who reign in life are those who have received two gifts, the gift of righteousness and the abundance of grace. Receiving the abundance of grace is the same as maintaining our confidence in Christ. It is coming to the cross at the beginning by faith and being saved by grace. It is coming to the living Christ day-by-day by faith and being saved by grace. It is acknowledging and demonstrating our dependence on Him, *not only at the cross but also in the crises.*

Hebrews 3 goes on to state that God's people, in the days of Moses, never entered into the rest God had for them: "So we see that they could not enter in because of unbelief." (v. 19). The tragedy today is this exactly, why many Christians never experience the rest God has for them. They never rest because they never reign in life, and they never reign in life because of their unbelief in the living Christ. They condemn themselves to a wilderness experience when all the time God has made a full provision for day-by-day living, day-by-day victory, and day-by-day rest in the indwelling Christ.

Where do you fit into this picture? If you sense a need in your life, why not do something about it, *while it is called today?*

4

Finding the Missing Security

I am beginning this chapter by quoting freely from an essay written by a seventeen-year-old boy in Christian high school. This boy had five years of instruction in the school. The title of the essay was, "On the Union of Believers with Christ." As you read, check your own ability to handle such an abstract subject. Suppose you were seated at a desk, given many sheets of paper, and allowed two hours to write on the subject. What would you have done?

"Before we consider the basis and existence of the union of Christ with His believers, we want to see whether this union is necessary as the goal to which God called man out of chaos, whether it is a condition of human nature, and whether man can bring it about by himself. . . .

"When we look at history, mankind's great teacher, we find that some nations may have achieved the highest level of culture, have given birth to the greatest men, have allowed their arts to flourish in full sunshine, and have developed a science that solved the most difficult questions; yet history adds with its iron pen that none of these nations was ever able to shake off the chains of superstition. None ever acquired the true and worthy concepts either of itself or of God. In fact, there never has been a nation whose ethics and morality were free from foreign additions and ignoble limitations. The virtues of the nations are not the products of a striving after true achievement, but rather are products of a crude and brutal bigness, a boundless egoism, a desire for glory and bold deeds. . . .

"Likewise, if we examine the history of man's nature as an individual, we constantly observe that the spark of divinity in his breast, the enthusiasm for what is good, the struggle for wisdom, the longing for truth, are being smothered by the flame of desire and greed. The zeal for virtue becomes deafened by the tempting voice of sin, and turns into a mockery as soon as we feel the full impact of life. . . .

"The striving toward understanding is pushed aside by a vulgar lust for earthly goods. The yearning for truth is deadened by the sweet flattering strength of the lie. Thus man remains the only creature in nature who has not fulfilled his purpose, the only member of the created universe who is unworthy of the God Who made him. . . .

"Yet the gracious Creator was incapable of hating His own handiwork. He wanted to raise it up to Himself, and so He sent His Son, and causes us to be called through these words: 'Now ye are clean through the word which I have spoken unto you. Abide in me, and I in you' (John 15:3–4). . . .

"Our hearts, reason, history, the Word of Christ, all call out to us loudly and convincingly to tell us that union with Him is absolutely necessary; that without Him we would be rejected of God; that He alone is able to deliver us. . . .

"Once a man has attained this virtue, this union with Christ, he will await quietly and composedly the blows of fate. He will bravely oppose the storms of passion and endure undaunted the rage of the wicked. For who can crush him, who can rob him of His Redeemer?" (quoted from *Decision Magazine;* August, 1969; Harmon Place, Minneapolis, MN).

There is, of course, much more material in the whole essay, but I have quoted this much for one special reason. When I first read this I was greatly impressed. Every time I read it I am amazed at what this young man knew. I'm sure you are wondering who he was. He is dead, and these words were written some years ago. Did he become famous? Yes, very famous. Was he a great preacher? Very much so. Who was he? His name was Karl Marx. Yes, *the* Karl Marx!

"But," you say, "this was written by a Christian." No, not necessarily. But what he wrote was true; indeed it was, and is. What Marx wrote was what he had been taught, and his answer was excellent. When he wrote answers for history and geography they would be equally good. He had a brilliant mind, able to assimilate facts and present them.

He knew what he was writing, but *knowing isn't believ-*

ing. Nowhere in his essay did he identify himself with what he wrote. When he left this school in Germany, he turned his back on God and embraced godless atheism. He went to London, England, where he studied and wrote his masterpiece *Das Kapital*. This book is the bible of Communism. Through him the Communist Party was formed. Lenin and Stalin were his protegees.

In one sense, the boy who wrote the truths about Christ is responsible for all the suffering, agony, and tragedy brought in through Communism. No one who has ever lived has caused more suffering in body, soul, and spirit than the boy who said: "The virtues of the nations are not the products of a striving after true achievement, but rather are products of a crude and brutal bigness, a boundless egoism, a desire for glory and bold deeds"—how crude, how brutal, how boundless!

One thing needs to be said at this point. Just imagine what would have happened if the teachers concerned had counseled with Marx and led him to trust Christ as his own personal Savior. The churches of Christ would have gained a tremendous theologian, and there would not have been a Communist Party! How great a door turned on the hinge of that young man's unbelief. Those of us who work with that age group should never take for granted the certainty of a person's belief, however much they know and however well they express themselves, because *knowing isn't believing*.

Marx found no security in Christ, but look with me at the writings of another man who found all the answers in Christ. We know him as Paul. He, too, was one of the world's brilliant brains. Unlike Marx he started out by persecuting the Christian faith, but he ended his life by dying for the Christ he once denied.

The second letter of Paul to Timothy is the last recorded writing we have from his pen. As he wrote, he was under sentence of death, expecting any day to be taken out for execution. In 2 Timothy 4:6–7 he wrote: "For I am now ready to be offered, and the time of my departure is at hand. I have fought a good fight, I have finished my course, I have kept the faith."

In the eyes of the world he was an utter failure; he had sunk to the lowest depths of hopeless disgrace. But in the eyes of heaven he was a supreme success. Even as he wrote, the Angelic Reception Committee prepared to greet the noble martyr on his entry into heaven.

The certainty and security that filled his mind are clearly set forth in 2 Timothy 1:12: "For the which cause I also suffer these things: nevertheless I am not ashamed: for I know whom I have believed, and am persuaded that he is able to keep that which I have committed unto him against that day."

Marx *knew*, but he did not *believe*. Paul knew *Whom* he had believed. Now where do you fit in? Many Christians with whom I counsel know *what* they believe, and this is why their problems develop. They know *what* they believe, but they do not know *Whom* they believe. This point is worth considering; it may help you in your situation.

I meet many people, including pastors and missionaries, who know what they believe. Their theology is excellent. If they were faced with an examination concerning the facts of the faith, they would achieve excellent results, all based on *what* they believe. But, it is possible to have a lot of "what," and still be fearful and insecure. Knowing what I believe is excellent; this should be a criterion for every Christian. Such knowledge gives confidence in discussion and provides authority in questioning; but of itself it fails to provide that intimate personal security which is missing in many lives today.

The difference between knowing "what" and knowing "Whom" is basically simple and follows from the previous chapters in this book. Knowing what concerns the saving death of Christ, the cross, and the precious blood of Christ, forgiveness of sins and certainty of a home in heaven. It is absolutely essential to pursue this knowledge and to be convinced of it. But, notice that knowing about the saving death of Christ is basically knowing *about* Him.

Knowing Whom I believe is based on an intimate and personal relationship with the living Christ and is concerned with the outcome of His saving life. Knowing Whom brings an effective present tense experience to my salvation, whereas knowing *what* takes care of the past and the future.

It is God's will that I should live my Christian life based on the glorious fact that I am complete in Christ. Completeness includes both His saving death and His saving life, both the *what* and the *Whom*.

But, to return to Paul's glorious words in 2 Timothy 1:12, as we face this question of the missing security, look once more at what he wrote: "I . . . am persuaded that he is able to keep that which I have committed unto him." In other words, Paul says, "He keeps what I commit." This is really the whole secret of knowing the quality of security which is missing from so many lives.

If I commit a thing to Christ, then He guarantees to keep that which I yield to Him. If I do not commit the area to Christ, then I choose to retain responsibility.

There are three areas in which we live, with which we are connected—the past, the future, and the present. Our hope of security, or lack of it, depends upon how we have, and are, committing these areas to Christ.

When we first responded to the gospel and came to Christ seeking forgiveness of sins, we were really committing to Him the whole question of our past. We acknowledged our need, our inability to handle the situation of our sin and guilt. We committed it to Christ at the cross, by faith, and He assumed all responsibility. As a result, we have complete security as far as the question of sin and guilt is concerned. No true believer loses sleep at night wondering whether Jesus paid it all. We know our sins are gone, because we have committed that area to Christ.

If you are reading these words and you have not personally trusted Christ as your Savior, then you are in extreme danger. You may be a good churchgoer, an excellent parent or child, but if you have not personally been to the cross and committed to Christ the whole question of your sin and guilt, then you have chosen to retain the responsibility for these areas yourself. Your sins remain unforgiven, because you have chosen not to commit them to Christ. You will go on living in your sin. You will die in your sin. You will be raised in your sin. You will stand before the Great White Throne still in your sin. You will eventually go to a lost eternity in your sin. All this because He keeps what I commit; but if I choose not to commit it to Christ, then I retain the responsibility.

When we came to Christ at the cross we committed to Him not only the past, but also—whether we realized it or not—the future. He has guaranteed to us a home in heaven. We can claim for ourselves His words in John 14:1–3:

> "Let not your heart be troubled: ye believe in God, believe also in me. In my Father's house are many mansions: if it were not so, I would have told you. I go to prepare a place for you. And if I go and prepare a place for you, I will come again, and receive you unto myself; that where I am, there ye may be also."

This security for the future is the heritage of every true believer. No one whose faith is established in Christ loses sleep at night wondering whether He will get to heaven. His Spirit bears witness with our spirits that we are the children of God and that someday we will see our Father in heaven.

We have spoken, so far, of committing to the Lord Jesus the past and the future in our lives. In one sense we knew all about this, because this is what we called "being saved." But the missing security in many people's lives is not the past or the future, but the present. We have seen that no real Christian has sleepless nights over the past and the future assurance of salvation, but—and here is the problem—there are many Christians, too many, who lose sleep because of the present tense in their lives. You may be one who looks to tomorrow, or next week, and is fearful as to the outcome. You know you should know better, and behave better, but the thought of tomorrow fills you with apprehension and frustrating insecurity.

You may be like one mother to whom I spoke recently. She talked of all her insecurity, of her fears and problems. They were like old friends, or old enemies.

She knew each one by sight and by name. She told me how she took them all to the Lord in prayer. But she did not realize that what *really* happened was that she carried her sack of troubles to the Lord, let down her sack, took out all her problems, spread them out before the Lord, and told Him all about them. Then, at the end, she put them all back in the sack, put it over her shoulder, and returned to her life just as burdened as ever with her present tense of trouble.

Telling the Lord about my present problems is not the same as committing them to Him. I do not carry around with me the guilt of the sins cleansed at Calvary. They are gone forever, because they were truly turned over to Christ.

How then do I go about committing to the Lord Jesus the present tense of my life? Basically, I follow the same line of thinking as I did with my sins and my future.

When I considered my sins and their guilt, there was nothing I could do about them. In no way could I help the Lord to die on the cross; in no way could I help to forgive my own sins. It had to be *Jesus only,* there was no other way. Thus it was that I left it all with Jesus, as the hymn says.

In like manner, I could not help the Lord prepare a place in heaven. There was absolutely nothing I could do with regard to the future. So once again I left it all with Jesus because there was no other way.

We need to follow exactly the same pattern of thinking with regard to the present, but this is where we fail. We tell the Lord about our situations, then we continue trying to worry our way through. How effective has your worrying been in solving your problems? Just think how much good worry you have wasted, mental effort which could have been used for other things!

So, it has to be once again, Jesus only—and committing means taking burdens there and *leaving* them there. I need to prepare my thinking as I speak to Him. I need to tell Him of my situations most certainly. Then I need to tell Him that I can do nothing about them. Own up to the fact that you are licked, don't be ashamed of admitting it. He knows about it even more than you do!

Tell Him you cannot handle the problems and then in the same breath say, "Lord Jesus, I can't, but Lord Jesus, you can!" Assure both the Lord and yourself that this is so. Then tell Him you want to commit it all to His keeping.

As you continue your daily life, the thoughts and doubts and fears over your problems will surely return. Expect them, and when they crop up again remind yourself and the Lord that these have been committed to Him. If the doubts return a hundred times, then a hundred times in quiet assuring prayer thank Him that all is committed to His care.

There is the initial act of committing it to Him, but this must be followed by the continual activity of committal. As we saw in the previous chapter, "We are made partakers of Christ, if we hold the beginning of our confidence stedfast unto the end." Committing the present day-by-day is partaking of Christ, appropriating all that He is for all that we need. Remember, the alternative to living this moment-by-moment yielded life is to blunder on doing what is "right in our own eyes." This latter choice condemns us to constant insecurity. It brings no blessing into our lives, it provides no joy and power for witnessing, and it certainly produces no glory to the Lord.

God's plan is so simple in its design, so logical in its

outworking, so positive in its success. And yet we choose to accept *part* of the plan and reject that which is our only hope of peace and rest day-by-day.

> "I know whom I have believed, and am persuaded that he is able to keep that which I have committed unto him against that day" (2 Tim. 1:12).

Do you really know what you believe? This is your hope of eternal security.

Do you really know Whom you believe? He is your hope of present peace, present power, and present security.

5

Finding the Missing Walk

Each summer for the over thirty years I attended Christian conferences across the U.S. both as speaker and hearer. These have been conferences for children, high schoolers, college students, young marrieds, adults, and families. So many times I have heard speakers stress the same vital need to every group. The language used depended on the age group, but it always boiled down to this: less talk and more walk; turn belief into behavior; let the world around you see you, as well as hear you; let your Christian walk match up to Christian talk.

Everyone realized the necessity for this. Everyone agreed that this should be so. Many went away determined to do their best to correct their failures. But in spite of all the definite agreement and the desire to put the determinations into practice, it wasn't many days or weeks before good intentions had disappeared and the old behavior patterns once more were in evidence.

Why should this be so, in spite of all the earnest hopes and desires? One of the reasons is that we have plenty of exhortation but not enough explanation! Our hearers are encouraged to mend their ways—to which they heartily agree—but so few of them are ever told *how* to do that. As well as the right message, they need the right method, presenting the right mechanics of the missing walk.

This chapter will set out to present these three things: the *truth*, the *technique*, and the *test*.

First, let us hear the challenge from the Word of God. Paul's letter to the Ephesians presents the highest realm of Christian truth. From what he said, we can see the excellence of the church there. The Ephesians were mature in the things of the Lord, but even so there is a repeated emphasis on the need for a walk which is in keeping with their beliefs.

Ephesians 4:1–3 presents Paul's urgent plea following his prayer for them concerning the indwelling Christ: "I Therefore, the prisoner of the Lord, beseech you that ye walk worthy of the vocation wherewith ye are called, With all lowliness and meekness, with long-suffering, forbearing one another in love; Endeavoring to keep the unity of the Spirit in the bond of peace."

Chapters 1, 2 and 3 unfold the glorious purposes of God for His people. They tell of the inheritance which is ours even now in Christ. They set forth the amazing change in our standing before God, from being dead in sins to being seated together in the heavenlies in Christ Jesus. The greatest possible privilege and blessing for us is detailed in 3:17: "May Christ through your faith [actually] dwell (settle down, abide, make His permanent home) in your hearts!" (AMP).

And now, because of all this blessing, and through his new capacity for living, comes the challenge to walk worthily, to match up to who we are and what we now possess. This was the positive presentation of what to do. In Ephesians 4:17–20 we find the same challenge, but from the negative aspect:

"This I say therefore, and testify in the Lord, that ye henceforth walk not as other Gentiles walk, in the vanity of their mind, having the understanding darkened, being alienated from the life of God through the ignorance that is in them, because of the blindness of their heart. Who being past feeling have given themselves over to lasciviousness, to work all uncleaness with greediness, But ye have not so learned Christ."

The opening verses of the chapter tell of who and what they were in Christ. These latter verses remind them of who and what they were when they were cut off from the life of God.

I find it remarkable that these words should need to be written to such wonderful Christians. With all the thrilling and exciting newness and nearness of the gospel, with men like Paul who had actually seen the risen Lord, we might imagine that they would be so much above the possibilities of failure. This, of itself, can be a great encouragement to us. Not only do *we* need the exhortation to walk worthily; even those so near Christ and His newly formed church were in similar need.

Chapter 5 picks up the same theme in the first verses: "Be ye therefore followers of God, as dear children; And walk in love, as Christ also hath loved us, . . . But fornication and all uncleanness, or covetousness, let it not be once named among you, as becometh saints". (vv. 1, 2a, 3). Notice the emphasis: Walk in love.

Verse 8 has these words: "For ye were sometimes darkness, but now are ye light in the Lord: walk as children of light."

Notice how these three positive references to our walk build on each other. The first was a walk of lowliness, the second a walk of love, and now this third one is a challenge to walk as children of light. Lowliness is the inward look, love is the upward look, and light is the outshining of it all.

Verse 15 of chapter 5 opens a section of vital teaching which leads on to a practical application: "See then that ye walk circumspectly, not as fools, but as wise. Redeeming the time, because the days are evil. Wherefore be ye not unwise, but understanding what the will of the Lord is." (vv. 15–17).

This is where the crunch comes. I am challenged to walk in the wise manner which demonstrates the will of the Lord. But the section does not leave it there, hanging as it were in mid-air. It goes on to tell us (v. 18) what the will of the Lord is. I am finding this eighteenth verse to be an increasing challenge in all my speaking. This is where so many of us miss the will of the Lord in our daily walks: "And be not drunk with wine, wherein is excess; but be filled with the Spirit."

The first half of the verse presents no problems. We all agree that to be drunk with wine is not the way a Christian ought to walk. It does not require much wisdom to see this or much difficulty in obeying the will of God in this area.

The second half is where the real problems lies: "Be filled with the Spirit," or, as the Amplified Bible puts it: " . . . ever be filled and stimulated with the [Holy] Spirit." This latter translation brings out the fact that it is not just a big crisis experience of being filled with the Spirit, but a day-by-day experience. It can begin with the crisis, but it is to be continuance of fullness.

This is the only place in the Bible where we are commanded to be filled with the Spirit. But, what I find most challenging is to see what follows, as the direct result of this being continually filled. There is no reference to speaking in tongues, nothing whatever of a charismatic connection. The proof and the purpose of being filled is seen in human relationships—husbands and wives, parents and children, management and labor.

But—here is the biggest question—what does it mean to be filled with the Spirit? I have found this to be the biggest area of failure in Christian lives. For many years I have dealt much with this topic, and I have been amazed to find the ignorance of so many "mature" Christians in this matter.

After all, this is the crux. If I do not understand what the Lord means when He commands me to be filled with the Spirit, then in no way can I obey His will. As a result, my walk will be incomplete, uncertain, unwise, and my daily Christian life will be marked with failure because it is based on ignorance.

Let us dig deep and find out what it means. First, let us see what it does *not* mean. It does not mean my having more of the Spirit. Being filled with the Spirit is not starting off with a small dose then increasing it as we go on. The Spirit does not come in different sizes pints, quarts, and gallons!

It does not mean my having more of the Spirit; it means *the Spirit having more of me!* Let me explain. I believe that little children can give their hearts to Christ at an early age. Our four children came to Christ before they were nine or ten. Others, I know, have trusted Him when they were four or five. This does not mean that they understood fully what they had done. Many adults are still uncertain in this area, but they opened up their hearts to let Him in. One of the loveliest things in all this world is the simple faith of a little child who has accepted what God gives.

The human heart is the human personality. The heart of a little child is, of necessity, a small area of experience and involvement. But when a little one opens his heart to the Lord Jesus, he lets Him into that small area of experience and involvement. In a very beautiful way such a child could be filled with the Spirit. The Lord indwells us in the person of His Holy Spirit. Being filled with the Spirit is being filled with Christ, so that when the Lord comes into the life of such a child He fills the tiny area to His own glory.

Now, here is where the trouble begins. When that five-year-old reaches ten or eleven years of age, the heart or personality is much larger. Such a child has had many more experiences, and his capacity for living now is on a much wider scale. In his relationship with the Lord he does not to be saved again, but he does need to yield to the Lord those new areas in his life.

Likewise, as he grows on through his teens, his lifestyle is completely changed and expanded. The tragedy I meet is that of a seventeen-year-old who seeks to be a Christian with the dedication of a five-year-old. When I speak to such a one, he tells me he trusted Christ when he was five, which is true. He is saved, but he is not being filled with the Spirit. His first-year-old area was filled by Christ, but now he has many other areas in his life. His new appetites, desires, ambitions, areas of friends all need to be yielded to Christ so that He can fill them.

This is where the battle begins. Such a boy can react against the idea of yielding his life to Christ. He was saved as a child, he has a home in heaven, why can he

not live his life his own way? This is where the devil
loves to step in and influence the boy to continued rebellion. Such young people get a warped idea of the
Christian life. I have come across this again and again
as I have counseled with them. To some of them the
Christian life is a kind of medicine you take. It is un-
pleasant, but you need to take it because it does you
good. The less you take the happier you will be! The
whole thing is a negative experience.

They fail to see that when we come and yield our
hearts and lives to Christ, He never takes away anything that is good for us. He always adds to the personality. If a boy is interested in sports, he will be a better
sportsman. If music is his joy, he will be a better musician. If art, a better artist.

Being filled with the Spirit is allowing Christ to move
into all the areas and outreaches of life. It is immensely
practical and has tremendously far-reaching effects.

The same situation applies to adults. A few years ago,
at the end of a week of meetings in a church, one of
the deacons came to me. His conversation went something like this:

"I am a medical doctor, thirty-five years old, and for
the first time I have realized what is wrong with my life.
I trusted Christ when I was eleven. He came into my
heart and filled my life.

"Now here I am, thirty-five years old, trying to serve
the Lord with the dedication of an eleven-year-old. No
wonder my Christian life is unbalanced and out of fo-
cus."

He had realized that in the intervening twenty-four
years his *heart*—his personality, the areas of his contact
and involvement with the world—had widened to a
vast extent. He saw himself now as a large area of per-

sonality, and right in the center was the small circle that he had yielded to Christ when he was eleven. How could he possibly be filled with the Spirit in such a situation? He saw that so much more of his life needed to be opened up to the Lord: his profession, his friends, his hobbies, his finances. This was the will of God for him, that Christ should move into all the new unopened areas.

We can almost work out the mechanics of being filled with the Spirit. See it this way: What I yield to Him, He takes; what He takes, He cleanses; what He cleanses, He fills; what He fills, He controls and uses.

If I hold on to certain areas in my life then the Lord cannot take them, cleanse them, fill them, control or use them. The Lord will not force His way into my life, just as He did not force me to trust Him at the cross. I was saved when I chose to come to the cross as a sinner and open up my heart to receive all the blessings of His saving death. I will continue to experience the daily presence and power of the risen Christ in my daily walk as I open up the closed and hidden areas to His presence.

Basically, the whole thing is profoundly simple, but terribly challenging. This is what the Lord meant when He said:

> "If any man will come after me, let him deny himself, and take up his cross daily, and follow me. For whosoever will save his life shall lose it: but whosoever will lose his life for my sake, the same shall save it. For what is a man advantaged, if he gain the whole world, and lose himself, or be cast away?" (Luke 9: 23–25)

Notice carefully that the Lord was not here talking about "coming" to Him, but "following" Him. In other words, this is the walk of a Christian. "Taking up his cross" does not mean putting up with the problems of life. I heard one man say that his cross was his mother-in-law. No such thing! A cross was designed for one purpose only, to die on! As I take up my cross, I am dying to self. I am releasing my hold on the control of my life; or, as we have seen above, I am *yielding* my life to Christ. Notice the use of the word *daily* in verse 23.

As we saw before, there is the act of dedication when I open my heart to Christ, but this must be followed by the *activity* of dedication. As I go on in my Christian life walking with the Lord, He by His Spirit and through His Word will show me things in my life that need putting right, areas that I have not yielded to Him. My job then is to yield those areas to Him so that He can take, cleanse, fill, control, and use.

This is why Ephesians 5:18 said: " . . . but ever be filled and stimulated with the [Holy] Spirit" (AMP). It is a lifetime's work. No one ever is fully filled. Not even Paul was satisfied with his relationship. The greatest saints who have ever lived have been most conscious of their need for deeper involvement with the living Lord.

You may be one of those earnest Christians whom I meet so often. You love the Lord. You want to serve Him. Your constant prayer is, as the hymn writer puts it:

"O use me, Lord, use even me,

Just as Thou wilt, and when, and where."

You want the Lord to use you, but your prayer is never answered. Can you see now why the Lord does not use you? He uses what He controls, He controls what He has cleansed, He cleanses what He takes, and He takes what we yield. If we haven't yielded our lives to Him, then He cannot fully use us in His service.

Realize, too, that being filled with the Spirit is being controlled by the Spirit. Controlled is the key word. I have come across those who claim to be filled with the Spirit whose daily lives are a demonstration of uncontrolled living. Being filled with the Spirit is being filled with Christ, being controlled by Christ. The obvious result of this will be, as we saw in 2 Corinthians 4:11: "that the life also of Jesus might be made manifest in our mortal flesh." Not I, but Christ.

The life of Christ which is made manifest includes the fruit of the Spirit in our lives. See this in Galatians 5:22–25:

> "But the fruit of the Spirit is love, joy, peace, longsuffering, gentleness, goodness, faith, meekness, temperance: against such there is no law. And they that are Christ's have crucified the flesh with the affections and the lusts. If we live in the Spirit let us also walk in the Spirit."

Notice it is *one* fruit, not *the fruits* of the Spirit. Compare this with verse 19: "Now the works of the flesh." There are many works of the flesh, but only one fruit of the Spirit. This nine-fold fruit is actually a picture of Christ, the life of Christ made manifest. It is His love, His joy, His peace, His longsuffering, His gentleness, His goodness, His faith, His meekness, and His temperance. And, as verse 25 says, "If we live in the Spirit, let us also walk in the Spirit."

There, once more, is the missing walk. Living in the

Spirit comes when I am filled with the Spirit, filled with Christ, with every known area yielded to His control.

My doctor friend made a wise decision which has changed the whole pattern of His living. When did you trust Christ? What area of your life is not under His control? Do you want to do the will of God?

6

Finding the Missing Rest

One of the most elusive commodities in the world today is *rest*. People will travel tremendous distances to find it. Others will make great sacrifices to come under its peaceful presence.

Some time ago I saw an advertisement in a magazine for a conference center, away in the backwoods. It said: "This conference has everything—*no* telephones, *no* radios, *no* TV." All was in search of rest.

Just as the world searches for this rest, the Bible presents the Lord as the One who offers it. Hebrews 4:9 says, "There remaineth therefore a rest to the people of God." It is still there, still available. Verse 11 offers a challenge: "Let us labour therefore to enter into that rest, lest any man fall after the same example of unbelief." We have to work at it. Only one thing can keep us from this rest: unbelief.

Once we have discovered the art of resting in the Lord, a new series of experiences can open up for us. I have found with some people an improvement in their health as they learn to rest, almost as if resting were part of a divine healing (which it is).

Many seek it, all believe in it, but how does a Christian learn to rest?

Let us begin our search by turning to Exodus 33:

12–14. This passage tells of one of the most personal interviews between the Lord and Moses, an interview that changed Moses' life. Previous to this section is the whole story of Moses—his birth, his failure, his running away, then the new era in his life when he met the Lord. It continues with the account of the miracles in Egypt, the Exodus, the crushing victory over Pharaoh, and finally the people all delivered, safe and sound, exactly as the Lord said He would.

"Operation Exodus" ended, and Moses faced an unknown future into an unknown land:

> "And Moses said unto the Lord, See thou sayest unto me, Bring up this people: and thou hast not let me know whom thou wilt send with me. Yet thou hast said, I know thee by name, and thou hast also found grace in my sight. Now, therefore, I pray thee, if I have found grace in thy sight, shew me now thy way, that I may know thee, and I may find grace in thy sight: and consider that this nation *is* thy people."

Moses here asks the Lord two questions: "Who is going with me?" and "Which way do I go?" In no way was he refusing to lead the people; it was help he wanted in these two areas.

In "Operation Exodus" he had the help of his brother Aaron, who had been raised all his life in Egypt, and who was knowledgeable as to places, people, and customs. But for this coming adventure Aaron would be useless. He knew nothing of wilderness ways. He was a city dweller. Hence the question: who is going with me?

Secondly, Moses wanted to know which way to go. Egypt was a civilized country with roads and recognized places, so that directions could be given and understood. They even had maps in Egypt. But now he faced the wilderness, with his back to civilization. There were no roads, no places to go to, no points of reference. Exodus 12:37 tells us there were "about six hundred thousand on foot that were men, besides children." Verse 38 says: "And a mixed multitude went up also with them." Six hundred thousand men, plus as many women, equals 1,200,000. With their large families there could have been more children than adults. These all, plus the mixed multitude, must have numbered *over two million people!*

So, here was Moses, with possibly two million ex-slaves, facing an unknown future in an unknown land. The responsibility was enormous. Consider the question of the daily water for them and the equally important question of the daily disposal of refuse. But Moses was not shirking the task; he simply wanted answers to his two questions.

God's answer to Moses was the most perfect answer for him, and for us, and for all time. No one but God could have suggested such an answer, and have been capable of carrying it out. The answer: "And He said, My presence shall go with thee, and I will give thee rest" (33:14).

What a glorious answer, so simple and so profound. Moses had asked first, "Who is going with me?", and the answer was, "I am!" God did not entrust the tremendous task to any human being, or even to an angelic being. He Himself was to be with them wherever they journeyed.

Moses' second question was, "Which way do I go?"

God's reply to this request was the perfect, supreme answer: "I will give you rest." In other words, the Lord gave Moses this complete answer, "I am going with you, and that is all you need to know!" Moses was to find rest in the God Who was always there. No need to ask, "Which way?" The pillar of fire was the guide by night, and the cloud the guide by day. As the cloud moved, so they followed—like the Wise Men who followed the star. The star brought them to where the baby Jesus lay. The cloud was the outward manifestation of the divine Presence.

So Moses started the rest of his life, forty more years, on the promise of God. Moses had many more questions and problems to bring to the Lord in the days to come, but never again did he ask who or where. He simply turned with quiet confidence to the Lord Who never left him nor forsook him.

Sometime ago I read those last words in God's answer to Moses, "and I will give thee rest." Here was God the Father speaking. Then my mind went to the words of the Lord Jesus in Matthew 11:28: "and I will give you rest." The same words, hundreds of human years later, spoken by God the Son.

I want us now to examine the whole of the speech from the lips of Christ, in which He, too, made that great promise. These words of Jesus give us the answer to "the missing rest." If you look and long for rest, this may be the end of your search.

First, we should make sure in our minds what *rest* really is—and what it is not! God promised Moses rest; God kept His promise, and Moses enjoyed rest. But the rest he enjoyed was not idleness. Moses never sat around doing nothing. How could he with more than two million people looking to him for every decision?

He was the President, the Senate, the House of Representatives, the Supreme Court, all rolled into one. He was on call twenty-four hours a day, three-hundred-sixty-five days a year. He lived in the midst of his people. He could never get away. No, the rest Moses enjoyed was *the conscious presence of the Lord,* Who Himself was the answer to every problem and burden. Moses learned to take it to the Lord in prayer, and he did not have far to take it! The proof of this is the fact that when the Lord eventually took Moses out of this scene, "And Moses was an hundred and twenty years old when he died: his eye was not dim nor his natural force abated" (Deut. 34:1). What a wonderful specimen of humanity! A hundred and twenty years old, able to read and write without glasses and able to climb mountains and endure the severest forms of physical testing. This was the physical perfection of a man who rested in God for forty years with never a day off, because resting in God was to him, in one sense, relaxing in God.

Expect the rest offered by Christ to be a similar experience. Let us see the whole of His discourse: "Come unto Me, all ye that labour and are heavy laden, and I will give you rest. Take my yoke upon you, and learn of Me; for I am meek and lowly in heart: and ye shall find rest unto your souls. For My yoke is easy, and My burden is light" (Matt. 11:28–30).

These are some of the most beautiful words in the English language. Those of you who are familiar with Handel's *Messiah* will almost hear the music as you read the words. The language is beautiful, the cadence is perfect, but the truth is blessed beyond words.

Consider the first verse: "Come unto Me all ye that labour and are heavy laden, and I will give you rest."

Let me ask you two questions: Did you come to Christ? Yes, you say. Have you true rest in your heart and life day-by-day? No, you say. Then what has gone wrong?

This is the mystery of the missing rest. How is it that for many true believers there is no rest in their hearts, only turbulence, unrest, fear, anxiety and frustration? Has the Lord run out of rest and blessing? Obviously, no! Then why is the rest missing when the Lord made His promise? This is what we will find as we read on and study these verses.

First of all, in verse 28 the Lord did not say, "You will find rest." He said, "I will *give* you rest." The fact that He offers rest and the fact that we enjoy that rest are two different things. It was the same situation when I first heard the gospel as a young man in my twenties. Every time I heard the message, the Lord was offering to me forgiveness and a home in heaven. But because I *heard* the message did not mean I was saved. There had to be a day when I came to the Lord in repentance and I *accepted* what He was giving; then I was saved.

One of our main problems is that we take a verse out of context and try to build our faith on that one verse. The truth spoken by Christ is in the three verses (28–30) and not only in the first verse. He did not *only* say, "Come unto Me."

Check through the three verses and you will find that Jesus gave a series of instructions which finally ended with the words, "Ye shall find rest unto your souls." There are four words to be obeyed, not one. The Lord Jesus said: Come, Take, Learn, Find. This is so simple, but so profound. If I fulfill only one of these conditions, I can never hope to achieve success. Let us look at all these words one by one and then, possibly, you may find "the missing rest."

The first word is *come*. This is the word with which we are familiar. Most of us have already accepted Christ as our Savior, and we understand the terms of the gospel. The second word is where the big challenge begins: *take*. "Take my yoke upon you." As I travel, I find this is one of the most neglected areas in Christian living, and possibly the least understood. Look into these words now with me.

First of all, the Lord said, "Come," and we came to Him. Now He says, "Take My yoke upon you," and most of us do nothing about it because we have no idea what He meant. The people to whom these words were first spoken would have had no difficulty in understanding the illustration.

We know that Jesus used simple everyday things to illustrate His messages. He spoke about the birds of the air, the flowers of the field, sunrise and sunset, the sower of seed, plus many other examples with which His hearers would be familiar. The words, "Take my yoke upon you," describe a situation commonly seen in that country. I never realized what it meant until I went to the Orient and to India. There the peasant farmers still use oxen for plowing in many cases. When the soil is soft and nonresistant, as in the water-logged paddy fields in the Orient, one animal is sufficient to pull the plow. But when I was in India I saw conditions similar to those in the Holy Land in the Lord's time. The soil was hard and stony, but even so the farmer had to break up that cruel earth before he could sow his seed.

There I saw the oxen being used in pairs. The proper term is "a yoke of oxen," the same word as in our verse. The yoke was simply a sturdy wooden bar which fit on the neck of the animal. The one bar was long enough to fit over the two necks, which were then fastened to the yoke. When the yoke is new it is rough and hard to wear, but as the years go by it becomes smooth and more easily adapted to the neck.

One of the common sights I saw was an ox, or water buffalo, at work with its calf running alongside. The mother might pull a cart or a plow while the young animal trotted at her side. She was available to satisfy his thirst whenever necessary. The calf was free—no ropes, no yokes. His need of his mother was the strongest tie!

But there comes a day in life of every calf when he is just too big to run around doing nothing. The farmer eagerly awaits that day, for then he has another source of power. It is a happy day for the farmer, but not so for the animal. For the first time in his life he has to take the yoke. Until then he has been gloriously free. His whole life has been "eat, drink and be merry," but then everything has to change.

I saw such a moment in action. The young animal was sturdy and strong and was enjoying his freedom, but he was brought to a place where an experienced adult ox patiently stood with a yoke on his neck. The newcomer refused to bow his head and submit to the new bondage. Then the farmer, plus his helpers, "encouraged" the rebel to humble himself with successive blows from hard sticks. This he eventually did, and that was the end of his "freedom." His life no longer was his own. He belonged to another, who could now do with him exactly as he pleased.

This is what the people listening to the Lord would fully realize. That is the way life was lived in His day. This is where we miss the whole point of His truth. The Lord says, "Come unto Me," and we gladly come and find freedom from sin. Then He says, "Take My yoke upon you," and we do nothing about it! We choose to run around "doing our own thing," just like the young animal did. Because we do not understand the teaching of the Lord, we do this in ignorance.

But, ignorance or not, the fact remains that so few are willing to submit to the yoke. Even when we understand His message, something within us rebels at the idea of yielding up our "freedom" and of committing our lives to the "bondage" of faith.

What we fail to realize it that this is the way it goes! Animals have to submit. That is why the farmer raised them. We *need* to take the yoke. This is God's plan of salvation. God never saved us so that we could run around "free." We were saved to serve. We have been bought with a price (1 Cor. 6:20). We are not our own!

The most interesting part of the illustration is what follows. In a yoke of oxen, one is always the leader. It is his yoke, and he leads while the other follows. The leader is older, more experienced, and has learned the simple techniques of pulling. Now, see what the Lord Jesus said: "Take my yoke upon you." Notice to whom the yoke belongs. It is *His* yoke, not yours. Later on in Matthew 16:24 the Lord says, "If any man will come after me, let him deny himself, and take up his cross, and follow me." This is a different picture. Each one of us has his own cross, as we saw in the previous chapter, but here in the eleventh chapter of Matthew, the yoke belongs to Christ.

See the wonder of His words. He is still "under the yoke," still seeking and saving that which is lost. He is Jesus Christ, the same yesterday and today and forever, still on the job. What He needs are others to help Him in the great task of reaching the lost.

This is the meaning of His call down through the

ages, "Take my yoke upon you. Come and join me in the greatest task of all." The tragedy is that many of us are eager to spread the gospel, to work and witness for Him—*our own ways!* We have our own plans, ideas, and techniques, and so we work at these, all in a good cause; but as a result we have no rest. Even the best of us can be driven on by a restless urgency. It may look good and sound better, but it is not what the Lord planned. He said, "Come and submit your whole life to me—your will, your hopes, and your ambitions. Take my yoke upon you."

Now, think back to our illustration and see why the young animal was lined up alongside the leader. The answer is obvious: so that he could learn the ways of life. The leader also was his teacher. To begin with he would find his new life restrictive, and he would want to go his own way. But the "persuasion" of the farmer with his big stick would beat him into submission. Eventually, when he had learned the art of submission, he could then go on to learn the way of life as it applied to him.

This is the picture the Lord applied to us: come, take my yoke, learn of me. When we come and take the yoke, His yoke, we too will find it restrictive in many areas. The flesh always wants its own way at all times. But if we can see the truth of the teaching and fit ourselves into the pattern, then blessing is inevitable both for us and the Lord. As we learn *of* Him and *from* Him, allowing Him to be both our leader and our teacher, then the promise of the Lord will come true in our daily lives: "Ye shall find rest unto your souls."

God's promise to Moses was, "My presence shall go with thee, and I will give thee rest," and Moses rested in the fact of the God Who was always there. "I will be with you; that is all you need to know!"

The promise of Christ to us is just the same. "I am with you alway, even unto the end of the world" (Matt. 28:20). Hebrews 13:5 (Amplified Bible) underlines the certainty of His promise: "For He [God] Himself has said, I will not in any way fail you nor give you up nor leave you without support. [I will] not, [I will] not, [I will] not in any degree leave you helpless nor forsake nor let [you] down (relax My hold on you)! [Assuredly not!]"

But I do not find the rest until I come, take and learn. As we saw, if I only come and never take His yoke and learn of Him, then I condemn myself to a restless Christian experience.

See also what the Lord said in Matthew 11. "I am meek and lowly in heart: . . . For my yoke is easy, and my burden is light" (v. 29a, 30). Then realize the implications. If He is meek and lowly and I learn of Him, then my life will become more Christ-like. His yoke is *easy*. The original word for *easy* signifies "fit for use, able to be used"; hence, good, virtuous, mild, pleasant, in contrast to what is hard, harsh, sharp, and bitter. The yoke of Christ is the fellowship of Christ—that which unites and binds us together in love. This is in comparison to the bondage of sin with its relentless agony of restlessness.

His burden is light. If I see myself in the picture, under the yoke, alongside the Lord, pulling together with Him, then it is obvious that my share in the work is light. It is *His* power, *His* peace, *His* plan, and I make myself available to Him. I abide in Christ and in doing so I find rest, and the peace of God which passes all understanding will fill my heart and life.

7

Finding the Missing Priority

Some years ago I had the privilege of traveling within the country of Taiwan to minister the Word of God to churches, schools, conferences, missionaries, and national pastors. One of the most strategic weeks was spent with a combined group of missionaries and national pastors. This was a unique occasion, the first time these two groups had ever combined for their annual conferences.

During the week I had many opportunities for speaking and counseling with individuals. To me, the most valuable time was spent with an American missionary. He was in his thirties, eager and willing to serve the Lord, but he had one tremendous problem.

As he told me his story it sounded like this: "I am in my mid-thirties. I came to know the Lord just a few years ago. I became very interested in missions and felt sure the Lord was calling me to Taiwan.

"I was a successful businessman, but I left all that I might serve the Lord Jesus. I have been through missionary training. I came out here a year ago, and I have spent this last year learning the Chinese language. I have finished my studies. I have my first appointment. I am due, in two weeks' time, to go south near Taejung. But . . ." He paused as he searched for words to describe his feelings. "But I've run out of steam! I simply cannot go on with it." He paused again and then said, almost in desperation, "I cannot go back home. That would be failure. But I cannot go on. I left everything to serve the Lord, and now look at me! What can I do?"

I am glad to report that during the week the Lord really spoke to him and showed him where his real problem was and how to put it right. I am sure that by now he is on the job doing a magnificent work for the Lord.

I have found that his problem is not unusual. He simply had his priorities in the wrong order. "Nothing very big", you say. No, it wasn't a tremendous problem, but it was enough to cause a breakdown in the ministry of a man of God.

His real failure lay in what was indicated by the words he repeated. He said, more than once, "I have left everything to serve Jesus."

"But surely," you say, "this is the proper thing to do, a noble act. What can possibly be wrong with leaving everything to serve Jesus?"

Let me tell you the story of the most successful missionary who ever lived. Let us learn from his own pen what was his first priority in his service for the Lord. His letter to the Philippians was written from prison. Fortunately for us, Paul spent many years in prison. Because of his prison experiences, we today have his ministry in written form. If he had been free, he would have gone and spoken the words. Because he was imprisoned he had to write them; hence, our blessing.

In Philippians 3 we read Paul's report on himself. In other letters also he presented his credentials as a minister of the Lord. In some cases churches had written to him to tell him about the wonderful visiting preachers they had heard, almost as if the visitors were so much better than Paul. He was almost forced to vindicate himself. See how he describes his background in verses 4–6.

> "Though I might also have confidence in the flesh. If any other man thinketh that he hath whereof he might trust in the flesh, I more: Circumcised on the eighth day, of the stock of Israel, of the tribe of Benjamin, an Hebrew of the Hebrews; as touching the law, a Pharisee; Concerning zeal, persecuting the church; touching the righteousness which is in the law, blameless."

In the eyes of a Jew, Paul's background was impeccable. He had all the basic history of an ordinary Jew, plus so much more. He was a "Hebrew of the Hebrews." He belonged to the tribe of Benjamin. These were the great fighters. He was a Pharisee. He says elsewhere that he was also the son of a Pharisee.

We tend to look down on the Pharisees because of what the Lord said about them. In His eyes they were full of failure and responsible for much of the deadness in the faith of the Jews. But, in the eyes of the ordinary people, the Pharisees were superior beings. They were special, first-class, super-citizens. They were treated with great honor and respect. To be a Pharisee and the son of a Pharisee put you right at the top of the totem pole!

In the eyes of the law, Saul of Tarsus was blameless. In the eyes of the people he was super-special. In the eyes of the high priest, Saul was a very up-and-coming young man. You will remember how he went to the high priest who commissioned him to go to Damascus and arrest any Christians he could locate (Acts 9:1–2).

He also had the distinction of being educated at the feet of Gamaliel. This is an indication of the high quality of the education he had received, equivalent today of going to the finest university.

This, then, was Paul—or Saul, as he was called prior to his meeting the risen Lord on the road to Damascus. He had everything he wanted in life. All he had to do now was to keep in with the right people and success was inevitable. There is no doubt that, with such a tremendous brain and intellect to follow through on all his social, material, religious, and educational assets, he was certain to reach the top of the religious world of his day.

But not only was the way open to success in the Jewish world, Paul was equally gifted in the political world. Remember, Paul was a Roman citizen. There is an exciting incident recorded in Acts 22:27–29 which illustrates perfectly his assets in this other sphere. Paul was in Jerusalem. He was mobbed by a crowd of fanatical Jews determined to kill him. Fortunately, the Roman chief captain—the commanding officer in the Roman garrison—heard of the riot and rescued Paul. As Paul was about to be scourged, he mentioned his Roman citizenship and was therefore called before the commanding officer for questioning.

What a contrast they would present! Paul, bruised and beaten, in torn clothes, standing before the officer in his spotless shining uniform. "Then the chief captain came, and said unto him, Tell me, art thou a Roman? He said, Yea. And the chief captain answered, With a great sum obtained I this freedom. And Paul said, But I was free born."

Here was the captain telling how much it had cost him to buy his Roman citizenship, but Paul could draw himself to his full height and utter those majestic words: I was free born! Not only was he a Pharisee and the son of a Pharisee, he was also a Roman and the son of a Roman!

Because of his Roman citizenship, this other world also was open to him. History records many instances of Jews who became powerful in the Roman world, in government, in finances. Paul, with his superb intellect, could have gone on to achieve fame and fortune in this other sphere.

In one sense he stood where two ways met. He could go the religious way and achieve the highest honors, or he could go the Roman way and realize all the glory of success.

Now, see what his response is in Philippians 3:7: "But what things were gain to me, those I counted loss for Christ. Yea doubtless, and I count all things but loss for the excellency of the knowledge of Christ Jesus my Lord: for whom I have suffered the loss of all things, and do count them but dung, that I may win Christ."

See how he lumps together all the potential honor of the Jewish world and all the future glory of the Roman world, and he calls them "things"—three times he uses that term. See how he turned his back on his future world and left all for Christ Jesus.

Now compare the words of my missionary friend in Taiwan with the words of Paul. They both had turned their backs on the material world. The missionary said, "I left everything to serve Jesus." Paul said in verse 10, "That I may *know* him, and the power of his resurrection, and the fellowship of his sufferings."

Notice the difference in their priorities. The mis-

sionary left everything to *serve* Jesus. Paul left everything so that he might *know* Jesus. If you check in the
life of Paul after his conversion on the road to Damascus, you will find that he vanished for two years. Where
he went we do not know, what he did we know not, except that he was "knowing Christ and the power of His
resurrection."

This is why Paul was such a glorious success as a missionary. He *knew* the living Christ and His risen power
in his life. This is why my missionary friend had run
out of steam. He did not know the living Christ nor His
risen power in his life.

My friend had been truly saved. The message of the
gospel had changed his whole direction. He was willing and eager to serve the Lord, and this he had
done—until he ran out of steam. He knew all about
the death of Christ, but he knew nothing experientially
of the saving life of Christ. He was seeking to live *for* Jesus; it seemed the right and proper thing to do. The
more he failed, the more his guilt increased, and the
harder he tried—until he ran out of steam.

Now, measure his experience against the experience
of Paul as recorded in verses 10–11:

> "[For my determined purpose is] that I
> may know Him [that I may progressively be-
> come more deeply and intimately acquainted
> with Him, perceiving and recognizing and
> understanding the wonders of His Person
> more strongly and more clearly], and that I
> may in that same way come to know the
> power outflowing from His resurrection
> [which it exerts over believers], and that I
> may so share His sufferings as to be continu-

ally transformed [in spirit into His likeness even] to His death, [in the hope] That if possible I may attain to the [spiritual and moral] resurrection [that lifts me] out from among the dead [even while in the body]." (AMP)

Paul's first priority in his life was that he might know *the Person* of the risen Christ, and then *the power* of the risen Christ in his daily experience. As a result, he went on to achieve his purpose and to become one of the greatest Christians who ever lived.

In previous chapters of this book we have considered the supreme importance of *knowing* Him as well as knowing *about* Him. See, in this specific case, how vital it was.

There are many Christians who run out of steam in their daily lives. In most cases the prime cause is "the missing priority." They fail to know the risen Christ and to experience His power in their daily lives.

Look with me at the second half of Paul's great desire: the *power* of the risen Christ in his life. It is possible to be knowledgeable in the truth of Christ indwelling us without experiencing the power or demonstrating His presence in our daily lives. Paul's prayer was that through the power of Christ, "I may so share His sufferings as to be continually transformed [in spirit into His likeness even] to His death, [in the hope] That if possible I may attain to the [spiritual and moral] resurrection [that lifts me] out from among the dead [even while in the body]."

There was a purpose in experiencing the power. He wanted a changed life, to be able to demonstrate to the world a spiritual and moral resurrection that would lift him out of the deadness of the world around him.

This is what my missionary friend needed—the Person and the power for the purpose. This is what each of us needs. This is what the world needs to see, people whose priorities in life produce transformed personalities.

Look again at the desire of Paul to experience a spiritual and moral resurrection that would lift him out from among the dead. See what he meant, and realize that this is vital in our lives, day-by-day.

When we come to Christ in repentance and seek His forgiveness and cleansing, we are saved, born again. In one sense we also experience a spiritual resurrection, then and there. The Holy Spirit puts it this way in Ephesians 2:1: "And you *hath He quickened*, who were dead in trespasses and sins." We were spiritually dead, but we have been quickened, or made alive.

In this sense, every believer has had a spiritual resurrection. Otherwise he still would be dead in his sins. But—and here is the big problem—not every believer has had a moral resurrection! Notice that even Paul, the great one, was still searching for a fuller experience of moral purity. He underlines this in Philippians 3:12: "Not as though I had already attained, either were already perfect: but I follow after, if that I may apprehend that for which also I am apprehended of Christ Jesus."

Paul was not perfect; he never would be. But his great longing was that he might experience more and more of what Christ had for him.

Everyone of us, whoever we are, needs more and more to experience an increasing moral resurrection in our hearts and lives. Most of us will agree with this, and as a result will set to work to live better lives. It seems the natural thing to do! That is exactly what it is, the *natural* thing. But we are not tied to the realm of the natural. Because we are partakers of the divine nature, we also can live in the realm of the supernatural.

The moral resurrection comes when I open up more areas of my life to the presence and power of the risen Christ. As we saw before, what I yield He takes, what He takes He cleanses, what He cleanses He fills, and what He fills He controls and uses. When the Lord cleanses, then there is a moral resurrection in that area of my life. It is so simple, yet so demanding. Yet this is the missing priority: to know Him and His risen power, and to allow Him to move in and cleanse.

When the Lord was here on earth, He cleansed the Temple so that God's full purposes could be accomplished therein. First Corinthians 6:19 teaches us that each of our bodies is the temple of the Holy Spirit, which is in us. If we allow Christ to move into our lives, then a similar cleansing can come to us. The wrong sacrifices can be put right and the busy practice of money changing can be put in its proper place, outside the temple of God. Then, with the missing priority put right, we can press on to enjoy the sweetness of His presence and the daily cleansing of His power.

But realize, this knowledge demands my deepest desire and my fullest cooperation. It is not enough to be emotionally moved and be full of sincere enthusiasm. These are necessary, but there also must be, as we read before, a determination to know Christ: "[For my determined purpose is] that I may know Him." The emotions, the mind, and the will must be ready and available to the risen Lord.

8

Finding the Missing Purpose

So often we take things for granted. We follow the
pattern which we have developed over the years, cling-
ing to our formality, or informality, whichever the emphasis may be. We will do well to look into the New
Testament to recall the emphasis there.

Look, for example, in Acts 1:8 and consider the last
words spoken by the Lord Jesus here on earth. The
words were few, but they gave, in no uncertain way, the
plan and purpose for all the church for all the days to
come:

> "But ye shall receive power, after that the
> Holy Ghost is come upon you: and ye shall be
> witnesses unto me both in Jerusalem, and in
> all Judaea, and in Samaria, and unto the ut-
> termost part of the earth."

These words are well known and much quoted. But I
find they are used mainly with a missionary emphasis,
the stress being laid on, "unto the uttermost part of the
earth."

As I meditate on these words, I am impressed repeatedly with the realization that here are the last words
spoken by the Lord. They contain His whole plan for

the ministry of the church, but in many cases we have forgotten the simplicity in our search for the successful.

The Lord Jesus here talks about the future service of Christians, both as individuals and as organized groups. I want us to examine three aspects of this service: *the power for service, the plan for service, the pattern for service.* These are the essentials, as from the lips of Christ. Whatever other wonderful and exciting programs there may be in the outreach of a local church, if these three are missing—the power, the plan, and the pattern—then all else is just "churchianity."

Notice first that the Lord said, "Ye shall receive power," and then, "Ye shall be witnesses." *The power for their future service was not to come from past abilities and experiences.* They would be witnesses on the basis of what they were *to receive,* not on the basis of who they were or what they possessed.

This is very important. Just consider that these men to whom Jesus spoke had been with Him throughout all His earthly ministry. They had seen every miracle He had performed. They had heard every truth He uttered. They had lived with Him day and night for three years. But all that did not qualify them to be witnesses!

John 20:30 says, "And many other signs truly did Jesus in the presence of his disciples, which are not written in this book." John 21:25 adds, "And there are also many other things which Jesus did, the which, if they should be written every one, I suppose that even the world itself could not contain the books that should be written."

The Gospels give only a selection of the words and deeds from the Person of Christ; therefore, we only know of these few. The disciples were acquainted with all the "many other signs" and all the "many other things," but even these did not qualify them to be witnesses. The words of the Lord were simple and sure: "You shall receive," and then, "You shall be."

This can be a great encouragement to us. I meet folk who say, "If I only knew more about the Bible, I would be able to witness more successfully." That statement is correct, but if it is offered as an excuse for withholding our witness, it is false. It is not how much we *know* that counts, but how much His power is filling us and using us.

Simple research into the lives of many Christians produces the fact that most of them were most effective in their witness soon after they were saved. They knew so little that it had to be the Lord who led and guided. Later on as their knowledge increased their power for witnessing waned.

The power for service, then, comes from the presence of the indwelling Holy Spirit—Christ indwelling us in the Person of His Holy Spirit. How does this power operate? Let me illustrate. It was some years ago that America launched the first nuclear-powered submarine. At the time of the launching, Britain was building the first nuclear-powered electricity project. This also was one of the wonders of the age. Normally in Britain, the production of electricity is a dirty business. Freight cars of black coal arrive at the power stations. The coal is burned in furnaces to boil water. The steam is used to drive dynamos, which in turn produce the electricity. Day and night the smoke pours out of tall chimneys, and the cables carrying 33,000 volts stretch out over the surrounding area, borne on pylons.

At the time of the building of this first atomic power

project, at Calderhall, we lived not far away. The atomic plant was unusual in design and in operation. No endless lines of freight cars arrived there. There were no tall chimneys, because there was no black smoke. Everything was clean and pleasing to the eye.

It so happened that I was the speaker one week at our Capernwray Conference Centers in England. During that week I spoke to a guest, a fine Christian man who, I learned, was the assistant director of this new marvel.

Like many others, I was curious to find out how the huge atomic plant operated. One day in conversation I said, "Tell me, how do you produce the power at Calderhall?" My friend looked at me with a straight face and replied, "We don't produce any power!"

"Excuse me," I returned, "I drove past your place this week. I saw no black coal, no smoke, but I did see the pylons carrying the power cables."

"I'm sorry," he said, "But we do not produce power." Then I saw his eyes were smiling. "All right," I confessed, "I'll buy it. What is the catch?"

"There is no catch, because we simply do not produce the power. The power lies in the uranium. We did not produce that; it is all part of God's great plan of creation. We have learned the secret of taking the uranium and releasing the power which already exists. Using this power we are able to produce the electricity."

As I listened to his explanation I was quite excited. "Why," I cried, "this is exactly how the Lord works in our lives. The power is in the indwelling Christ. He indwells us. Our job is not to *produce* power, but to *release* a power which already exists."

He smiled and said, "Hasn't anyone told you that

the God of creation is also the God of redemption?" That was the title of my morning message!

When I realize that the power for service comes into my life when Christ comes in, at the cross, then the burden of struggling to produce the power is taken away. As we saw in chapter 7, I learn to rest in the presence and power of Christ who always is there.

Think back to the days of the early church. Try to realize what they did *not* possess. They had no church sanctuaries, no educational buildings. They had no conference centers, no camps, no VBS programs, no Bibles or hymnals, no seminaries or Bible schools— nothing that we would consider essential today. There is only one thing they possessed: POWER!

It was said of them that they turned the world upside down. Today the world turns the Christians upside down.

I sometimes meet groups of simple believers living in so-called backward areas of underdeveloped countries. They, too, have no "things" we deem essential, but they see the power of the Holy Spirit working in wonderful ways. Back home in the United States it is possible to see churches with the most magnificent buildings covering acres of ground, organizing the most comprehensive programs backed by an army of personnel. They have literally everything except power!

It is possible to organize the Lord Jesus out of His church. When He goes, the power goes!

Now, notice the plan for service (still in Acts 1:8): "Ye shall be witnesses unto me." These words are so few and so simple, yet they contain the secret of the success of the early church. We will learn that this is basically what is missing in much of our present-day evangelism.

"Ye shall be witnesses." One reason why we miss the full meaning of the plan of service is because we have a limited understanding of the word *witness.* We see, or hear of, many television programs based on cases in a police court in which the witness gives evidence. We are apt to limit the act of witnessing to the confession of one's faith, but that is not all. The original word translated *witness* is *martus* or *martur,* from which we get the word martyr, one who dies for his faith.

The Lord said, "You shall be witnesses"—you, the whole of you, your thoughts, words, and deeds. The way you talk, walk, dress, drive your car, behave in your home and at school or business. In every possible outreach of human communication, "You will be a witness of me!" This in itself is one of the big areas of failure, where the missing purpose is so evident.

I have been to churches where the pastor announced classes for training to witness. I was pleased to see the response of the people to his invitation. Now, just suppose the pastor had announced training classes being set up for those who wished to be martyrs. What a difference the response would be! Yet I have been to tribal villages in Vietnam, especially to Dame, where Christians died for their faith.

Some months before I arrived there, a band of Viet Cong had raided the village. They lined up the teenagers and mowed them down with machine guns. They stole all the food. They set fire to the miserable houses in which the people lived. The culmination of their evil was to take the five pastors and hang them in the door of their church. As these men of God were dying, the murderers took long knives and slit open their bodies. In doing so, they openly mocked and defied the Lord.

What moved me most was to see a new church being erected, and five new pastors on the job. Each man knew that the Viet Cong would return, and each knew what to expect. But these people were witnesses for Christ! Thank God, not many of us are called upon to pay such a price, but we are called to be witnesses in a full sense.

Then the Lord Jesus said, *"You* shall be witnesses unto *Me."* We have seen who the "you" is—all of our faculties. Now notice who the "Me" is. Who said these words? Christ did.

"Yes, but which Christ?" Realize that it was the *risen* Christ speaking. His instructions to His disciples were: "You will be witnesses unto *Me,* the risen, victorious Lord." They had to proclaim to a defeated, degenerate world the truth of, and the fact of, the risen Christ.

This again is another area in which the missing purpose is evident. Let us compare the preaching of the early Church with the evangelism of today.

Follow with me the simple story of the response of the disciples to the Lord's plan for service. In Acts 1:21–22, we see the first council of the early Church. It is an ordination committee seeking a successor to Judas.

> "Wherefore of these men which have companied with us all the time that the Lord Jesus went in and out among us, Beginning from the baptism of John, unto that same day that he was taken up from us, must one be ordained to be a witness with us of his resurrection."

Notice there was only one requisite for ordination. No inquiry was made into his education, or seminary, or degrees. Simply was he a witness to the risen Christ. How wonderful it would be today if every man who was ordained was a living witness to the risen Christ!

In Acts 2 we have the account of Pentecost and of Peter's great message to the crowd assembled there, from whom three thousand were to be added to the church later in the day.

As Peter spoke, he reached the climax of his message when he referred to the prophecy of David: "He seeing this before spake of the resurrection of Christ, that his soul was not left in hell, neither his flesh did see corruption. This Jesus hath God raised up, whereof we all are witnesses." (vv. 31–32). It was the witness of Peter to the risen Christ that made the hearers cry, "Men and brethren, what shall we do?"

Again in chapter 3 we have the story of Peter and John on their way to the Temple. The lame man is healed and the crowd gathers once more. Peter takes the opportunity to witness for Christ: "But ye denied the Holy One and the Just, and desired a murderer to be granted unto you; And killed the Prince of life, whom God hath raised from the dead; whereof we are witnesses." (vv. 14–15). Once more Peter was faithful to the words of Christ—"witnesses unto Me."

In chapter 4 we have the only picture of a perfect church. Verse 32 tells of their unity and the results of such perfect communal love. Verse 33 continues, "And with great power gave the apostles witness of the resurrection of the Lord Jesus: and great grace was upon them all." The two characteristics of this perfect church were great power and great grace. Would that every church today enjoyed a similar experience! Now notice what it was that produced these two outstanding blessings. *It was their witness to the risen Christ.* It was He, the risen Lord, Who supplied the great power and the great grace.

Chapter 5 records the imprisonment of the apostles, how the authorities laid their hands on them and put them in common prison. Verse 19 continues: "But the angel of the Lord by night opened the prison doors, and brought them forth, and said, Go, stand and speak in the temple to the people all the words of this life."

It was as if they were recommissioned with an added assurance. Notice what they had to preach: all the words of this life! The emphasis still had to be on the risen life of Christ.

We can pause here and compare, as suggested before, the preaching of the early church with much of the evangelism of today. As we already have seen, the culminating thrust in the emphasis of the gospel preached in Acts was the resurrection and the risen life of Christ, or as we have described it elsewhere in this book, the saving life of Christ.

Much of today's evangelism centers and culminates in the cross. The great emphasis is on the saving death of Christ with the gift of forgiveness of sins and a home in heaven. Thank God for every preacher and every message which uplifts the cross and glorifies the precious blood of Christ. But, if we *stop* at the cross, we do not fulfill the words of the Lord. He did not say, "You will be witnesses unto my death." The emphasis was to be on the Person of the risen Lord.

The early church preached the risen Christ. You cannot preach a risen Christ *without* preaching a dying Christ. Before you exalt His saving life, you must first present His saving death.

But, you can preach the cross of Christ *without* going on to the resurrection. You can preach His saving death without presenting the completed picture with His saving life. This is what evangelism does today. Thank God preachers call people to the cross, thank God for everyone who is saved by the death of Christ. *But,* if all they do is send the people out to "live for Jesus," they condemn them to a life of defeat and failure. This is the missing purpose of which we are writing.

We could continue in Acts and see how, repeatedly, the message preached was a complete message. Even in Acts 17 where Paul was preaching in Athens on the Areopagus the message was unchanged. He spoke to pagan philosophers and intellectuals, but he declared:

> "He hath appointed a day, in which he will judge the world in righteousness by *that* Man whom he hath ordained; *whereof* he hath given assurance unto all *men,* in that he hath raised him from the dead. And when they heard of the resurrection of the dead, some mocked: and others said, We will hear thee again of this *matter.*" (vv. 31–32).

We have discussed the power for service, and just now, the plan for service. Let us look finally at the third emphasis: the *pattern for service.* We will learn this also from the life of the Lord.

John 12 records how the Lord had come to Jerusalem for the last time in His earthly life. Ahead of Him lay all the agony of Gethsemane and Calvary . In verse 24, the Lord spoke of this coming tragedy in an unusual way: "Verily, verily, I say unto you, Except a corn of wheat fall into the ground and die, it abideth alone: but if it die, it bringeth forth much fruit." He told of the basic rule for reproduction in the vegetable kingdom: "unless a seed dies it can never reproduce itself." He saw Himself as the heavenly corn of wheat Who was to die so that the glorious harvest might appear. In one sense, the Lord Jesus died so that He might never be alone.

This we know, and this we believe. But then in verse 26 the Lord continues, "If any man serve me, let him follow me." Make sure you really understand this basic pattern for service. If I want to serve Him, then I must follow Him. But notice where I first follow Him: *into the grave.* This is the whole point of this amazing illustration. If life is to come through me, in my service for Him, then I, too, must be willing to follow Him into the grave.

This is what Paul says in Galatians 2:20, "I am crucified with Christ"; not "I was" or "I will be," but a *continuing present tense experience* of identification with Christ in the place of death. He saw himself as dead for Christ's sake. But then he continued: "Nevertheless I live; yet not I, but Christ liveth in me: and the life which I now live in the flesh I live by the faith of the Son of God, who loved me, and gave himself for me."

There was a special purpose in Paul seeing himself dead with Christ. He wanted the indwelling Christ to take over in his life so that the life of Christ might be made manifest in his mortal flesh. In this way, the power would be released, fulfilling the power for service. Then Paul would be a witness for the Living Christ—in thought, and word, and deed—thus fulfilling the plan for service. Finally, he would be faithful to the pattern set for him by the One Who died so that we might live.

Is this purpose missing in your life?

9

Finding the Success of Failure

In our western world we have definite ideas about success and failure. Success means bigger and better; failure means the way down. Success is a positive thing, whereas failure is totally negative.

We are taught from our childhood that the greatest thing in life is success. It doesn't matter what you go in for as long as you succeed. But nobody tells us what success really is!

Does it really mean making a fortune? Getting power? Being praised? Beating your competitors? Is success supposed to bring happiness and joy, or is success for the sake of success?

How about the many men and women, young and old, who achieve success and then commit suicide? The millionaires, the pop stars, the film stars, the socialites—all so successful in the eyes of the world. Is this success?

By what standards can a Christian measure success? Does it mean a bigger church for a pastor, or, in our daily witnessing, more souls won for Christ?

The Bible teaches that *success is obedience to the will of God,* whatever the results may be! This is why, in an amazing way, failure can be success!

Check with me the lives of some of God's great ones

and see what success really meant for them. There is no doubt that they were great. Their names have rung out down through the centuries. But consider what really happened.

Deuteronomy 31 deals with the events leading up to the death of Moses. By that time he was 120 years old. The last forty years of his life had been totally devoted to the Lord. The struggle in Egypt had been followed by the long, drawn-out trials in the wilderness. During all these many years Moses had been God's man— spirit, soul, and body—every minute of every hour of every day! There had been no vacations and no time off.

In verse 16 the Lord told Moses what would happen when he died. He learned that all his years of devoted service would end—in failure!

> "And the Lord said unto Moses, Behold, thou shalt sleep with thy fathers; and this people will rise up, and go a whoring after the gods of the strangers of the land, whither they go to be among them, and will forsake me, and break my covenant which I have made with them."

All Moses' years of teaching and training were to end in utter failure. He had reasoned with them, cajoled them, threatened them, persuaded them. He had been tried and tested, despised and persecuted. The people had poured out their frustration and bitterness on him. And now, as he came to the end of his life he learned that these people, his people, were to turn away from the Lord, and all the years of struggling would be wasted.

See how he addressed them in verse 27: "For I know thy rebellion, and thy stiff neck: behold, while I am yet alive with you this day, ye have been rebellious against the Lord; and how much more after my death?"

What a sad situation, to look back over all the years, and to know for a certainty that the people with whom he had toiled so long were destined to failure. But this was not Moses' fault; he was not to blame. He had been utterly faithful to God, and so regardless of the results, this was success. The Lord God had known this, he had foretold it, and so, in a strange way, the failure of the work was the success!

Isaiah is another giant of the Old Testament. We know and enjoy him best because of the sixty-six chapters that bear his name. What a comfort and a challenge these writings have been down through the years! But Isaiah was also a speaking and preaching prophet as well as a writer for God.

Chapter 6 contains the awesome story of his call to the ministry. It begins with the vision he saw of "the Lord sitting upon a throne, high and lifted up, and his train filled the temple." He goes on to describe the seraphims, who cried one to another, "Holy, holy, holy, is the Lord of Hosts: the whole earth is full of His glory."

Isaiah then tells of his own reaction, how he cried, "Woe is me! for I am undone; because I am a man of unclean lips, and I dwell in the midst of a people of unclean lips: for mine eyes have seen the King, the Lord of hosts." (v. 5).

We read next how his lips and life were purged from sin and iniquity. Then comes the tremendous challenge from the Lord: "Whom shall I send, and who will go for us? Then said I, Here am I; send me." (v. 8).

This is an oft-told story full of inspiring truth. Generally, the teacher or the preacher stops reading at this verse. We are left to imagine what happened to Isaiah. As we associate him with the majestic verses of prophecy in the Bible, we are inclined to imagine that in his spoken ministry he had a similarly successful career.

Let me read on in this same chapter and show you what the Lord promised him:

> "And he said, Go, and tell this people, Hear ye indeed, but understand not; and see ye indeed, but perceive not. Make the heart of this people fat, and make their ears heavy, and shut their eyes; lest they see with their eyes, and hear with their ears, and understand with their heart, and convert, and be healed" (vv. 9–10).

What a promise! "You go and preach, but no one will understand what you are saying; no one will see the point of your ministry. Their hearts will get fat and lazy, and no one will respond and be healed."

No wonder Isaiah, in verse 11, cried out, "Lord, how long?" How long had he to continue preaching with no response? What a shock it must have been to him when he heard the Lord's reply: "Until the cities be wasted without inhabitant, and the houses without man, and the land be utterly desolate, And the Lord have removed men far away, and there be a great forsaking in the midst of the land." (v. 11–12). He was to go on preaching, with no response from the people, until the whole nation was completely turned away from God.

In other words, Isaiah was destined to see failure right from the beginning of his ministry. Just consider what you would do if you were in his position. You preach, but no one listens; you continue year after year with no response.

Was Isaiah a success when all he saw was failure? Would the world call that success? Realize that *Isaiah was not called to be a success; he was called to be faithful in that which the Lord had given him to do.* In his case once again, it was the success of failure.

Jeremiah is probably the greatest example in the Old Testament of such a ministry. For forty years he called Jerusalem and Judah to turn back to God. He warned them, giving accurate details of what would happen if they continued on their way. He said the glorious Temple of Solomon would be burned and Jerusalem destroyed.

But no one gave heed to his message. They scorned the ideas of the Temple and Jerusalem. The Temple was God's holy Temple, and Jerusalem was God's sacred city. He would never destroy His own holy places.

And so the years went by, almost like a countdown to destruction. Jeremiah was persecuted, punished, imprisoned, sentenced to death, but he lived on.

There came an awful day in his life when he walked through the streets of what had been Jerusalem. He saw everything come true as he had prophesied—the burned Temple, the destroyed city, the dead bodies in the streets. No one had listened to his call to repentance.

Was he a success? Forty years of preaching his heart out for God and no results. Is that success? Yes, one hundred percent success; because he was not called to convert a nation, but *to be faithful to the will of the Lord.*

Ezekiel had a similar experience of preaching with little success. In Ezekiel 3:4 we read: "And he said unto me, Son of man, go, get thee unto the house of Israel, and speak with my words unto them." The Lord continued in verse 7: "But the house of Israel will not hearken unto thee; for they will not hearken unto me: for all the house of Israel are impudent and hardhearted."

Ezekiel's reaction is shown in verse 14: "So the Spirit lifted me up, and took me away [in the vision], and I went in bitterness [of discouragement] in the heat of my spirit; and the hand of the Lord was strong upon me" (AMP). He was discouraged, but he was not disobedient. Once more his success was demonstrated by his failure.

One of the most interesting stories concerning this subject of true success is about a character of whom we know little, but whose reactions are so much like what ours would be. His name is Baruch, and he was the servant and secretary to the prophet Jeremiah. We meet him in Jeremiah 36:

> "And it came to pass in the fourth year of Jehoiakim the son of Josiah king of Judah, that this word came unto Jeremiah from the LORD, saying, Take thee a roll of a book, and write therein all the words that I have spoken unto thee against Israel, and against Judah, and against all the nations, from the day I spake unto thee, from the days of Josiah, even unto this day. It may be that the house of Judah will hear all the evil which I purpose to do unto them; that they may return every man from his evil way; that I may forgive their iniquity and their sin. Then Jeremiah called Baruch the son of Neriah: and Baruch wrote

> from the mouth of Jeremiah all the words of
> the LORD, which he had spoken unto him,
> upon a roll of a book." (vv. 1–4).

What a task that must have been for Baruch, day after day, patiently writing the messages on the roll of the book! Notice in verse 1 the order was given in the fourth year of the king. Verse 9 tells how in the fifth year of the king the roll was read. Many weeks had passed in the painstaking task of writing the words from Jeremiah's dictation.

Verse 5 tells that Jeremiah was "shut up," restricted from going to the house of the God. He may have been under house arrest because of the condemnatory nature of his preaching. He could not go, but there was no reason why Baruch should not go and read from the book of Jeremiah.

The chapter goes on to tell what happened when Baruch read, telling of the awful judgment to fall on Jerusalem unless the people repented. Verse 10 tells how he read: "at the entry of the new gate of the LORD's house, in the ears of all the people."

One of those who heard him reading was a man called Michaiah. He was so impressed that he reported the event to all the princes who were then meeting in the scribes' chamber in the king's house. Such was his report that the princes sent Jehudi to Baruch, saying, "Take in thine hand the roll wherein thou hast read to the people, and come." (v. 14).

Baruch arrived with the roll in his hand. He was told to sit down and read it to them. "Now it came to pass, when they had heard all the words, they were afraid both one and another, and said unto Baruch, We will surely tell the king of all these words" (v. 16).

They asked Baruch how he came to write it. He replied, "He pronounced all these words unto me with his mouth, and I wrote them with ink in the book" (v. 18).

Baruch was told to hide, both he and Jeremiah, and to let no one know where they were. Then the princes arranged for the king to hear these amazing words of warning. So far the people had given attention to them, and the princes had been filled with fear. Now, what would be the reaction of the king?

> "And Jehudi read it in the ears of the king, and in the ears of all the princes which stood beside the king. Now the king sat in the winterhouse in the ninth month: and there was a fire on the hearth burning before him. And it came to pass, that when Jehudi had read three or four leaves, he cut it with the penknife, and cast it into the fire that was on the hearth, until all the roll was consumed in the fire that was on the hearth. Yet they were not afraid, nor rent their garments, neither the king, nor any of his servants that heard all these words" (vv. 21–24).

How embarrassing for the princes to report to Baruch that the book he had spent so long in writing had been deliberately burned by the king! Not only so, but the king had ordered the arrest of both Baruch and Jeremiah. And so Baruch returned to Jeremiah to report both tragedies—the book burned and they themselves on the wanted list!

What happened next? The Lord spoke to Jeremiah once more: "Take thee again another roll, and write in it all the former words that were on the first roll" (v. 28). Now see the quiet obedience of Jeremiah to such a request: "Then took Jeremiah another roll, and gave it to Baruch the scribe . . . who wrote therein from the mouth of Jeremiah all the words of the book which Jehoiakim king of Judah had burned in the fire: and there were added besides unto them many like words" (v. 32).

Jeremiah had been the Lord's faithful, obedient servant for twenty-three years; he still had seventeen more years left before the destruction of Jerusalem. Patiently he began all over again. But how about Baruch, the man who did all the writing?

Chapter 45 contains just five verses. It seems to be out of place because it tells Baruch's reaction to the writing of the roll. "The word that Jeremiah the prophet spake unto Baruch the son of Neriah, when he had written these words in a book at the mouth of Jeremiah, in the fourth year of the reign of Jehoiakim the son of Josiah king of Judah". Notice when this incident took place, in the fourth year of the king. Comparing this with Jeremiah 36:1 we see that this occurred during the writing of the first roll.

Verse 3 of chapter 45 quotes some of Baruch's complaint: "Thou didst say, Woe is me now! for the LORD hath added grief to my sorrow; I fainted in my sighing, and I find no rest." Baruch was tired of the job, he found no rest, he was seeking a change.

The next two verses contain tremendous words from the Lord to him: "And seekest thou great things for thyself? seek them not: for, behold, I will bring evil upon all flesh, saith the Lord: but thy life will I give unto thee for a prey in all places whither thou goest" (v. 5).

To understand what God is saying we need to know some more information concerning Baruch. He came from a noble family. His grandfather was Maaseiah who had been the governor of Jerusalem under the great King Josiah. (See Jer. 32:12 and 2 Chron. 34:8). By birth he was entitled to honor and respect, comfort and ease. But some years back he had joined Jeremiah as his secretary and companion. In doing so he stepped out of his life of pleasure into the hard life of a prophet of Jehovah. As we saw, he was wanted by the police.

This is the man who, as the book was being written the first time, complained of being weary with the task. The Lord's answer to him was not to seek great things for himself, but to get a sense of proportion, to see himself involved in the eternal counsels of God!

To the credit of Baruch we can see that not only did he complete the first copy, he read it, risked his life in doing so, and when the book was burned he wrote it all over again. He truly raised his eyes from the commonplace business of writing words day after day to see himself involved in the eternal counsels of God.

The best part of the story is to realize that we have the words that he wrote; the book of Jeremiah. If there had not been a Baruch, humanly speaking, there would be no prophecy of Jeremiah in our Bible.

At first all that Baruch would see was failure. Then he experienced total failure in the fire. But, once again, the success of Baruch was his experience of failure.

All these men, and there are many more in God's Word, cry out to us that *success is not bigger and better.* Success can be a hopeless experience of failure. But if in doing the job we are obeying the will of God, that is success!

What can this mean to you? Oh, so much! Be like Baruch and seek not great things for yourself; get your eyes on the will of the Lord. See yourself, however small and insignificant, involved with the eternal counsels of God.

The Lord said to him, "Thy life will I give unto thee . . . whither thou goest." The Lord Jesus says to us, "My life will I give to thee . . . whither thou goest." "Lo, I am with you alway, even unto the end of the world."

Fill in the missing links. See yourself complete in Christ. Walk constantly being filled with His Holy Spirit. Find the missing rest. Break the silence barriers. Accept the privilege of suffering. And go on to know the peace of God which passes all understanding.

10

Finding the Missing Pause

There is a particular word that has been really lost in the reading and preaching from the Bible. It is a Hebrew word which occurs seventy-one times in the book of Psalms and three times in the book of Habakkuk. It has been there, in the pages of the Word of God, for thousands of years, but somehow it has been overlooked and neglected. I have never heard anyone preach concerning it. I notice that when people are reading aloud and come to the word they stumble over it, mispronounce it, or even omit it. Some modern paraphrases do not even put the word in its place; they just leave it out altogether.

I cannot imagine the Holy Spirit recording such a word seventy-four times, then preserving that word through all the years of Old Testament writing and copying, just to have it dropped in our day!

The word is *Selah* (se'-lah). It was probably a word of instruction for the musician. As in the case of the words, *Amen* and *Hallelujah,* it has remained untranslated—but it has a meaning. The Amplified Bible has rescued the word from obscurity and has put it this way: "Selah [pause, and calmly think of that]!" I have found that when I do what it says, when I pause and calmly think about the preceding passage, there is a message for my heart, at that time.

There is great emphasis these days on speed reading. I have been to several churches where special classes are held to teach and promote the art. I'm sure there are many advantages to be gained from such a skill, but the Lord did not invent speed reading! The emphasis in the Bible is on the word "meditation." It was one of the keys to the success of David in his relationship with God.

Reading is one-way traffic. My eyes go to the page and find what is there. Meditation is two-way traffic. My eyes go to the Word, and the Word comes back into my heart and my mind. *Selah* is applied meditation, taking the Word of God and allowing it to work in our hearts and lives.

With this idea in our hearts let us turn to Psalm 32 and practice the art of meditation as we become involved with the word *Selah*. This Psalm has eleven verses, and the Selah appears three times in those few verses. It helps to divide the meditation into three distinct progressions.

See how the Psalm commences: "Blessed is he whose transgression is forgiven, whose sin is covered. Blessed is the man unto whom the Lord imputeth not iniquity, and in whose spirit there is no guile." (v. 1–2).

This is a precious picture of a soul at peace with God. When the Lord looks at such a person, there is a unique quality of transparency—a freedom from sin and guile. The word translated *guile* means deceit, laziness, slothfulness.

This should be the condition of every believer, to walk humbly with our Lord always with a tender conscience towards sin, as we practice the truth of 1 John 1:9 so it can become personally real: "If we confess our sins, he is faithful and just to forgive us our sins, and to cleanse us from all unrighteousness."

Now notice how the next two verses of the Psalm (vv. 3–4) paint a very different picture. The quality of peaceful transparency as described in the first two verses is a rare thing these days. It is indeed God's plan for the normal Christian life, but in practice we all fall far short of the pattern. Our normal everyday living bears more resemblance to these next two verses: "When I kept silence, my bones waxed old through my roaring all the day long. For day and night Thy hand was heavy upon me: my moisture is turned into the drought of summer. Selah." (Pause and calmly think of that).

Here is the first Selah. I am thinking of it as *the Selah of conviction*. What happened in David's life was the result of the convicting power of the Holy Spirit. There is an inner sense of weariness and lack of youthful spontaneity. There is a daily groaning over all the situations of his life. There is a sense of God's hand against him and upon him. Verse 4 literally means "my life juices were turned into the drought of summer." His vitality was gone; only a dry unfruitful condition remained.

What an accurate picture this is of many of the people with whom I counsel! All the symptoms are there— weariness, deadness, dryness, and a sense that nothing is going right. Everything is going wrong, just as if God was against them!

Thus we have our first Selah: Pause and calmly think of that.

The reason for this miserable condition is clearly stated in the first four words of verse 3, "when I kept silence." It was the *silence* in the life of David that produced the wretched situation. I have found that very often silence can be more damaging and hurtful than spoken words. I remember one wife speaking of her husband's attitude: "If only he would curse me or scream at me, but all he does is remain silent."

It is this silence in the life of both the sinner and the saint that produces the buildup of inward misery. Perhaps some of you can look back on your own experiences before you trusted Christ as your Savior. You heard the message of the gospel. By the convicting power of the Holy Spirit, you recognized your need of Christ as your Savior. But then you put it off, tried to evade the issue, made many excuses for taking no action. It was during this time of noncommunication on your part that the misery set in. As the time went by, it became a day-and-night issue with you—the deadness, the groaning, the dryness.

The same thing happens in the life of a Christian. There could be some people reading these words who are guilty of this attitude of silence. There may be things in your life which have come between you and the Lord. As yet you do not call them sins. You have rationalized the acts or the situations, seeking to explain your present conduct to your own satisfaction. You have words of explanation for your behavior, and you are hiding behind this barrier in an attitude of silence.

As you continue in this act of self-deception, you will also move into this condition set forth in verses 3 and 4. God never planned that a Christian's life should be an arid experience of age with groaning and oppression as a daily diet. Only one thing keeps us there: sealed lips. A stubborn, silent heart of self-will is a wilderness of self-inflicted misery and hopeless despair.

But David did not stop there. There is a second Selah at the end of verse 5. I am calling this, *the Selah of confession*. This is the answer to the failure just discussed. "I acknowledged my sin unto Thee, and mine iniquity have I not hid. I said, I will confess my transgressions unto the Lord; and thou forgavest the iniquity of my sin. Selah." (Pause and calmly think of that).

The secret of blessing in such a wretched condition is to break the silence barrier. Some years ago, in the field of aeronautical science, the ultimate was to break the sound barrier. Eventually it was accomplished, and today it is an everyday occurrence. But in many of our lives the ultimate still needs to be reached—to break the silence barrier.

When David acknowledged his sin, ceased to hide his iniquity, and confessed to his transgressions, forgiveness followed freely from the heart of God. We can learn something here by examining the three words used to describe his failure: sin, iniquity, and transgression. Notice it is *sin* and not *sins*. The word *sin* describes the root principle in the heart of man. It is the comprehensive term for moral obliquity, the inward element which produces the acts, the natural attitude in the human heart. Transgression speaks of breaking the law. Iniquity is lawlessness or wickedness, a positive act of self-aggrandizement against the holiness of God, whereas transgression is a negative act of breaking specific commandments.

So we see that David began by acknowledging that in him was this thing called sin. Because of this, he was a sinner, and because he was a sinner, he committed sins. Some Christians have failed to realize this fact, that human nature is predisposed to go its own way, and it always will operate that way. Even as a Christian my human nature is not improved. God's salvation is not concerned in making people better or in improving human nature. Second Corinthians 5:17–18 clearly states, "Therefore if any man be in Christ, he is a new creature: old things are passed away; behold, all things are become new. And all things are of God . . ."

God is not in the business of patching up human lives. He wants to make totally new people, and He does this by sending into every Christian heart the gift of His Holy Spirit. In this way the Lord Jesus comes to dwell in our hearts in the Person of His Holy Spirit.

Follow the steps of David's confession. First, the open acknowledgement that in him was this principle of sin. Then openly showing his iniquity, his deliberate acts of self-will. He then confessed his transgressions, the many ways and times he had broken God's law and done specific deeds. The result was that God forgave the whole deliberate attitude of self-will springing from the sin resident within him. This is why it says, *Selah—pause and calmly think of that!* Amazing grace, how sweet the sound!

When I fail to realize the fact that sin indwells me and that my human nature *is* sinful and always will be, then I try and do better next time, or try harder to be a better person. Such a quality of living only prolongs the dryness and deadness. It is when I break the silence barrier and confess to the Lord my total inability to do anything of myself acceptable to Him—*then* the blessing comes.

Some will say, "That is correct for sinners when they come to the cross. They have to confess their sin and total failure." This is very true, but verse 6 of Psalm 32 goes on to say, "For this shall every one that is godly pray unto thee in a time when thou mayest be found."

This need to confess sin, iniquity and transgression is not only for the sinner, but also for the saint. *I am convinced that one of the greatest needs in our churches today is for believers to get right with God—this way!* There are too many silent saints withering away in their own areas of self-will and self-righteousness, justifying their own transgressions, and calling iniquity by other names.

The message was loud and clear in David's day. John repeated the same word in his day: "If we say that we have no sin, we deceive ourselves, and the truth is not in us. If we confess our sins, he is faithful and just to forgive us our sins, and to cleanse us from all unrighteousness." (1 John 1:8–9). The word *unrighteousness* here could also be translated "iniquity," as in Psalm 32, a deliberate act of self-will.

Notice how John was careful to include himself in this category. He did not say, "If *you* say . . . if *you* confess." Even with his many years of Christian experience (he was then over ninety years old), he still recognized his need to walk in transparent dependence upon the grace of God.

Look again at verse 9 and see the transcendent goodness of God. We are called upon to do one thing: to confess the sin principle within us and the resultant sins outflowing therefrom. If we do this, then God promises to do two things: to forgive and to cleanse. He does these two things because He is both faithful and just.

Because He is faithful, He forgives our sins in the courtroom of heaven. The precious blood of Christ is the propitiation, or mercy seat, for our sins (1 John 2:2).

But then, not only is He faithful; God is also just. If there is no record in heaven, then there must be similar treatment here on earth. That is why He cleanses us from all unrighteousness. We are forgiven in heaven and cleansed in our own hearts—all on the basis of breaking the silence barrier. A cleansed heart is a pure, transparent heart in which there is no guile.

Every real revival in the church down through the ages has come as a result of Christians getting right with God. The revival has begun first in the hearts of God's people, then it has overflowed to the world around. It comes not through widely advertised programs and emotionally built-up situations. The sacrifice of God still is a broken spirit. God will never despise a broken and contrite heart (Ps. 51:17). This was the experience in the revival in Southern Canada in the early 1970's. Christians broke the silence barrier, then God broke the blessing barrier.

There is one more Selah at the close of Psalm 32:7. We can call this *the Selah of consecration.* It comes at the end of the promises of added blessing to the one who has responded to the Lord: ". . . surely in the floods of great waters they shall not come nigh unto him. Thou art my hiding place; thou shalt preserve me from trouble; thou shalt compass me about with songs of deliverance. Selah." (Pause and calmly think of that.) (vv. 6b–7).

What a contrast this is with the misery of verses 3 and 4. There, the whole situation was insecure and most unsatisfactory. Now see the glorious security: *"Thou art my hiding place."* Because David saw himself hidden with God, other blessings followed. The floods of great waters could not rise to his place of safety. More than this, he was preserved from all trouble. Then God did something more; He built a hedge around him, a circle of song, songs of deliverance. Verse 10 adds more to this thought, *"But he that trusteth in the Lord, mercy shall compass him about."*

What a lovely idea this is! My Heavenly Father preserves and protects me. He builds, not a wall as with an enclosed city, but a twofold circle of songs of deliverance and the infinite overwhelming strength of the mercy of God.

Make sure you appreciate the tremendous gift of the mercy of God, leading to deliverance. Mercy is another forgotten word these days. Nobody wants mercy; *we want our rights.* This demanding of rights is the background to the rising fever of worldwide rebellion. But thank God for His mercy which surrounds us, and for His songs of deliverance which encompass us. As these two blessings combine, they set us apart for God Himself, and being set apart for God means being consecrated to Him.

And so this missing word *Selah* leads us in a sure progression, from conviction through confession to consecration.

The loveliest part of all is to realize that this sequence is not just a clever idea in theology; it is a real flesh and blood, day-by-day experience for each of us. And it begins by breaking the silence barrier.

11

Finding the Missing Privilege

We who are true Christians are a very privileged people. Regardless of race, color, education, or social status, we have amazing blessings—sins forgiven, a home in heaven, a heavenly Father who cares for us individually, a blessed Savior who will never leave us nor forsake us. How rich we are, how privileged!

There is one special privilege which is for each of us, yet when we hear of it, we turn away from it, to our great loss. You will find it in Philippians 1:29: "For unto you it is given in the behalf of Christ, not only to believe on him, but also to suffer for his sake."

There it is, the missing privilege: the privilege of suffering! Somehow we never look upon suffering in that way. Most gladly we accept the blessings of believing on Christ. We recognize these as a glorious series of positive advantages. Yet this verse tells us that through suffering we equally can be blessed. To us suffering is a negative experience, something to be avoided.

In some places I find Christians who are tremendously interested in divine healing. They will attend all kinds of meetings, travel long distances, and put up with many inconveniences—all in the interest of divine healing. Thank God for all the blessings that can come to us through such joyous experiences, but we should also remember that the Bible promises equal blessings through divine suffering!

I have met certain individuals whose lives are warped because they never have received divine healing. They have searched for it, claimed it, almost demanded it; but it never came, and so they became frustrated with God. Somehow it never seemed to have occurred to them to claim the other rich blessings from divine suffering.

I have been much challenged, in meditating on this subject, to see how important suffering was in the life of our Lord. Hebrews 2:10 is an amazing verse: "For it became him, for whom are all things, and by whom are all things, in bringing many sons to glory, to make the captain of their salvation perfect through sufferings."

This is a verse I cannot fathom or understand, and yet here it is in the Word of God that somehow, somewhere, for some reason it pleased the Father to make the Lord Jesus, the Captain or Leader of our salvation, perfect or complete through suffering. We know there is no sorrow, sin, or suffering in heaven, and therefore in one sense our Lord never came into contact with it in His divinity. But here on earth, not only was He the Son of God, He was also the Son of man.

He was to be treated in all points as we are. He was to be a High Priest who could empathize with us. And somehow the only way He could be made complete in His humanity was through suffering. Note, it was not *success* that made Him complete, but *suffering*.

Likewise in Hebrews 5:8–9 is another sentence that humbles me every time I read it:

> "Though he were a Son, yet learned he obedience by the things which he suffered; And being made perfect, he became the author

of eternal salvation unto all them that obey him."

Just consider this amazing statement. He was the Son of God—the pure, sinless, spotless Son of God—and yet He learned obedience through the things that He suffered. This is teaching me a tremendous truth, that there is one special way to learn obedience, and that is through suffering. Even the Lord Jesus had to learn it that way. He could say in John 8:29: "I do always those things that please him."

Two of the characteristics of our day are, first, the avoidance of suffering, leading to a constant desire to have everything the easy way; and second, a deep spirit of disobedience, leading often to a rebellious attitude. These two go hand in hand and are the exact opposites of what we are considering. They lead to a weak, ineffective quality of Christianity that is afraid to suffer, afraid to dare for Christ, and is concerned for the most part in being respectably uninvolved.

First Peter 2:20–21 is very helpful in this area:

> "For what glory is it, if, when ye be buffeted for your faults, ye shall take it patiently? but if, when ye do well, and suffer for it, ye take it patiently, this is acceptable with God. For even hereunto were ye called: because Christ also suffered for us, leaving us an example, that ye should follow his steps."

Jesus not only is the Leader, He is the Example for us to follow in the matter of suffering. The Amplified Bible, in the same verses, speaks of this suffering: "It is inseparable from your vocation." But we have the wrong attitude. We see suffering sometimes as a punishment from God, whereas the Bible says, "For whom the Lord loveth he chasteneth, and scourgeth every son whom he receiveth" (Heb. 12:6).

In some cases, human suffering can be a proof of the love of God. We never see it so at the time; we may never live to see it so in this world. But it is helpful to get our eyes away from the negative attitude.

I want us to consider the subject of suffering, the missing privilege, under two simple headings. First, *suffering is the source of our salvation.* I am writing these words at Easter time, and my mind has been much occupied with the events of the last few days in the earthly life of our Lord.

I have considered once more the scene in the garden of Gethsemane where the Lord Jesus faced up to a quality of suffering that was new, even to Him. He was going to bear our sins in His own body. As He bore our sins, He also was going to bear the guilt, because the burden of sin in the human heart is the guilt is brings. Second Corinthians 5:21 goes further and adds: "For he hath made him to be sin for us, who knew no sin; that we might be made the righteousness of God in him."

This is something we can never understand because we have a fallen human nature. Sin and guilt are part of our way of life; but Jesus was spotless and sinless. We can begin to appreciate the situation if we imagine ourselves truly guilty of some heinous crime—only one! How sick and horrible we would feel. How we would despise ourselves and feel so totally wretched and hopeless, with the guilt of one sin.

The Lord Jesus in Gethsemane faced up to bearing the guilt of *all* sin. As we saw above, *He was made sin,* almost as if He was so saturated in the sin and guilt that it absorbed His whole being.

With this impending awfulness, He knelt and said: "O my Father, if it be possible, let this cup pass from me: nevertheless not as I will, but as thou wilt" (Matt. 26:39). Notice that terrible word: *if, if it be possible,* if there is any other way whereby sin and guilt can be removed. Verse 42 continues the agony, "O my Father, if this cup may not pass from me, except I drink it, thy will be done."

It was almost as if the Lord Jesus in His humanity pled for a possible alternative; but all the time there was the ever obedient spirit, "nevertheless not as I will, but as thou wilt."

Luke 22:43–44 presents us with a picture that calls forth deep pity: "And there appeared an angel unto him from heaven, strengthening him. And being in an agony he prayed more earnestly: and his sweat was as it were great drops of blood falling down to the ground." So great was the agony of soul and utter exhaustion of His bodily frame that it needed the special ministry of an angel to enable Him to continue.

From these depths of weakness He went on to the trials, scourgings, and beatings—without rest, without sleep. Finally He was crucified. He refused the cup of myrrh which would have deadened the pain and clouded His mind. He bore our sins and was made sin—that fact which had tested Him in the garden.

Over seven hundred years before this event, Isaiah wrote, foretelling in chapter 53 the total inclusiveness of the suffering:

"He is despised and rejected of men; a man
of sorrows, and acquainted with grief, . . . he

> was despised . . . he hath borne our griefs,
> and carried our sorrows . . . he was wounded
> for our transgressions, he was bruised for our
> iniquities . . . he was oppressed, and he was
> afflicted. All we like sheep have gone astray;
> we have turned every one to his own way: and
> the LORD hath laid on him the iniquity of us
> all" (vv. 3–6).

Suffering is the foundation on which our salvation is built. We recognize this every time we take the Communion, sharing in the Lord's Supper by breaking the bread and drinking the cup. It was the Lord Jesus who said, "Do this in remembrance of Me." It was His desire that we should never forget the price He paid so that we might be free from the guilt of sin and delivered from the hopelessness of a lost eternity.

But then, not only is suffering the source of our salvation, it is also *the strength of our salvation.* This is why so many of us live weak and flabby lives, so opposite to what the Lord planned and desired.

The basic reason is that many of us look upon our salvation only as an escape from guilt and punishment. Thank God we are delivered from our just deserts, we who were the guilty ones. But true Christianity is *involvement,* not escapism.

We should become involved in the total plan of God. We were involved with the saving death of Christ and thus we were delivered. That is *the act of salvation.* But that is not all; there is *the activity of salvation,* by which we go on to live strong vigorous lives to His glory. The motivating power behind this activity is involvement through suffering.

We can see this perfectly displayed in 2 Corinthians

12:7–10. In the opening verses of this chapter Paul recounts the amazing experiences he had when he was caught up to the third heaven. These were such that: ". . . lest I should be exalted above measure through the abundance of the revelations, there was given to me a thorn in the flesh, the messenger of Satan to buffet me, lest I should be exalted above measure. For this thing I besought the Lord thrice, that it might depart from me."

As in the case of Job, God allowed Satan to move into the life and daily experience of Paul. The source of his suffering was "a thorn in the flesh," which was "the messenger of Satan." The verbs used to describe the resultant agony are in the present tense, indicating that the pain was ever present with all its weakening power.

It is interesting to understand the word which is translated "thorn" in verse seven. There are two words in the New Testament which are both translated by the one word, "thorn." The first is *akantha*, the word used the most. It describes the type of thorn found on roses and similar thorny bushes. This is the word used for the crown of thorns worn by our Lord.

The other word is *skolops*. It is only used once in the Bible, in this verse. It signifies, not a thorn as in the word *akantha*, but a sharp pointed stake. Such stakes are used to support young trees. They can be several feet long and are always sturdy and strong. This, metaphorically speaking, was the source of Paul's suffering—as if a long pointed stake pierced his body and protruded at each side.

The source of his trouble obviously was visible as well as painful. There have been many deductive suggestions as to what it might have been, but the Bible is

silent as to the actual affliction. This is just as well, because had we known the nature of the thorn it would,
in a sense, have limited our identification with Paul. As
it is now, we can take his experience and apply it to
each of our own lives.

Notice Paul's first reaction to his suffering. He
prayed and begged the Lord to take it away. He did
not ask for strength to deal with it, but for a total removal. As he agonized for an answer, no reply came
forth. Again he poured out his heart's desire to God,
and once more no answer came. The third time, he ap-
pealed for mercy and deliverance. Then God spoke to
him:

> "My grace is sufficient for thee: for my
> strength is made perfect in weakness." (v. 9).

Make sure you realize that this is God's eternal answer to *all* sufferers and to their sufferings.

As I think of Paul seeking deliverance from the
thorn, I am reminded of the Lord Jesus in the garden
of Gethsemane. Both of them prayed three times before God, crying out in agony (Matt. 26:44). Both were
seeking the removal of the source of their sorrow. The
answer to Paul, as we have seen, was that he was of
more use to God with the thorn.

There was no answer to the Lord Jesus, no word of
comfort, only an angel to enable Him in His humanity
to face further suffering. There was no answer to His
three prayers, and on the cross itself, there was no answer to His bitter cry, "My God, my God, why hast thou
forsaken me?"

In one sense, there was no need for an answer to His
cries of bitter sorrow, because the answer was given

long ago in Psalm 22. This Psalm begins with that same cry of brokenness and loneliness, but the answer is found in verse three, "But thou art holy, O thou that inhabitest the praises of Israel."

The holiness of God demanded the separation from the sin of man, even when it was being borne by His own beloved Son. This again was part of the awful burden on the heart of our Lord as He knelt in Gethsemane to face the darkness of separation.

I find this incident in the life of Paul a great help in understanding the subject of divine healing. Consider Paul as a most worthy recipient of such a blessing. Was he deficient in his faith? Obviously not, for he could say, "I can do all things through Christ which strengtheneth me" (Phil. 4:13). Did he not deserve to be healed? Obviously, yes. If any man was worthy of special treatment, Paul was that man.

Why was not Paul healed? The answer is that God had another plan for his life. Paul's reasoning was correct by human standards. His theory was: "The stronger I am, the more use I will be in the Lord's service. Only make we whole. Heal me and I will be more effective."

Then the Lord put forward His teaching on divine suffering. "The source of all strength in My service is My grace, which us unending and unlimited. And My strength is made perfect in your weakness, not in your strength. You are more use to me with the thorn and its resultant suffering."

Paul could then do one of two things. He either could reject the word of the Lord and continue to rationalize his situation, or he could accept the truth from the word of God, accept the thorn and all its continuing suffering, and look to a faithful God to provide that daily strength which would be made perfect in his weakness.

As we know, he took the latter course: "Most gladly therefore will I rather glory in my infirmities, that the power of Christ may rest upon me" (2 Cor. 12:9). This is the secret of success in dealing with this missing privilege. The key word is *acceptance,* accepting from the hand of God that which we did not choose, and did not desire, believing all the time that, as in the case of Paul, His grace will be sufficient for us and that His strength will be made complete in our weakness as the power of Christ rests upon us.

Paul went one step further in proving that suffering is the strength of our salvation: "Therefore I take pleasure in infirmities, in reproaches, in necessities, in persecutions, in distresses for Christ's sake: for when I am weak, then am I strong" (2 Cor. 12:10). Notice how this verse develops the breadth of Paul's acceptance. In the previous verse he was concerned with the thorn in the flesh, that which was physical pain. In this verse he speaks of the added areas of suffering and pain, such as come into our lives: infirmity, reproach, need, persecution, distress—things which are not only physical, but emotional or spiritual, and which test the human powers of resistance and endurance. Regarding these added trials he said he took pleasure in them because, "When I am weak, then am I strong."

Paul had learned, by experience, that by accepting from the hand of God the situation with all its trials and testings, he then moved into a new capacity for power and strength. It wasn't that he *enjoyed* the suffering, just for suffering's sake, but because suffering was a door. When he put the hinges of acceptance on the door of suffering, it opened wide into a glorious sense of the presence and power of Christ.

In the same way, an unusual treasury of blessing can be ours only through the door of suffering; but we, too, must supply the hinges of acceptance.

This is some of the richest teaching in the Word of God. It is so contrary to human reasoning, but history and experience substantiate it to the full. Our great need is to become involved in this missing privilege.

There may be some of you reading these words who are in special need. You may be holding back from some form of service because, in your eyes, you are not able due to some weakness—either physical, emotional, or spiritual. You have the desire to be used of the Lord, but like Paul you need your problems removed before you can see yourself in action.

As I write I can call to mind the names of people known to me now who are much used of the Lord in differing ways. But when I first met them and saw either their physical deformities amounting almost to ugliness, their defective vision or blindness, their stammering and stuttering tongues, their extreme age or youth, their inability to communicate, I wondered in my ignorance how the Lord could use such people.

I think of others whose background is sordid and unlovely—those with criminal records who have known sin and iniquity to the full. How could the Lord use them? Then the answer comes back every time: "My grace is sufficient for thee; for my strength is made perfect in your weakness."

Why don't you take these words to yourself? Take your failure, your suffering, your pain and hopelessness, and see it as God's special door for you. Put on it the hinges of your acceptance and see it open to the treasure house of His grace and His strength. Don't wait for the Lord to heal you, free you, or restore you. Don't fight your fears or your failure. Don't demand answers from the Lord. Come with a new song on your lips and a new prayer in your heart. Why don't you adapt this prayer to meet your own need?

A Prayer of Acceptance

Dear Father in heaven, I want to come to You in a new way.

I have come many times before asking, pleading, and begging that You would take this thing out of my life.

I have bargained with You, that if You would remove my "thorn," then I would be a better Christian and I would serve you more effectively.

Now, Lord, I want to come the way Paul did. I did not ask for this problem; I do not desire it even now. But if You can use me in this condition, then here and now I am willing to accept it from Your hands.

I accept, "the pain, the infirmity, the reproach, the needs, the persecution, and the distress for Christ's sake."

Heavenly Father, as I put the hinges of acceptance on the door of my sorrow and suffering, may it swing open in Your good time to the abundant treasure-house of Your grace and love in Christ Jesus.

May I go on to know Him in all His risen power in the midst of my tragedy and trouble.

Thank you, Lord Jesus, for all the promise of blessing which lies ahead of me, for all the days to come, as I accept this privilege of suffering for Your dear Name's sake."

Amen.